Graeme Wright is a former editor of *Wisden Cricketers' Almanack* (1987–92 and 2001–02). He is also the author of several acclaimed cricket books including *A Wisden Collection*, *Bradman in Wisden* and *Betrayal: The Struggle for Cricket's Soul*, which was described by the *Daily Telegraph* as 'outstanding, intelligent and observant' and by the *Spectator* as 'one of the most enlightened, thoughtful and disturbing books ever written on the game.'

BEHIND THE
BOUNDARY

CRICKET AT A CROSSROADS

GRAEME WRIGHT

Published in the UK in 2011 by A&C Black
An imprint of Bloomsbury Publishers Plc
36 Soho Square, London W1D 3QY
www.acblack.com
www.bloomsbury.com

ISBN 978 14081 2672 1

A CIP catalogue record for this book is available from the British Library.

Cover photograph © Photolibrary.com
Commissioned by Charlotte Atyeo
Edited by Rebecca Senior
Designed by seagulls.net

This book is produced using paper that is made from wood grown in managed,
sustainable forests. It is natural, renewable and recyclable. The logging and
manufacturing processes conform to the environmental regulations of the
country of origin.

Typeset in 10pt Minion by seagulls.net

Printed and bound in Great Britain by CPI Cox & Wyman

CONTENTS

ACKNOWLEDGEMENTS

Most likely this is not the book it was intended to be before I set out to research it. I was planning something more in the line of an audit of the business of professional cricket in England. What I hadn't anticipated was the degree of distrust and even anger around the first-class counties, levelled not always at the England and Wales Cricket Board (ECB), as may have been expected, but at each other. I hadn't appreciated that there was as much competition off the field as on it. Conflict was a word frequently recurring in my notes.

What surprised me also was the frankness with which those within the game were prepared to speak. It was as if they saw in this book a forum wherein they could express views, ideas and concerns for which there wasn't always the time, or even the encouragement maybe, when they got together at ECB meetings. In a way, then, this has become their book rather than mine, their opportunity to put their side of the story. And because county cricket has brought me many pleasant hours in good company, I was happy to let that story run. I just stuck my oar in from time to time.

Needless to say, none of it would have been possible without the generous input of a number of people, some of whom have since left county cricket. The game will be poorer for their absence. Cricket is not that big a business really, but it is more complex and more conflicted than seems imaginable when you're sitting at a county ground, thinking the only contest is that in the middle between bat and ball. Behind the boundary, the contest is more often one of passion v pragmatism, heart v head, and that's not even the half of it.

In particular, then, I am grateful to the following for their time, conversations and, on occasions, some very good cricket lunches: Keith Loring at Derbyshire, David Harker at Durham, David East at Essex, Tom Richardson at Gloucestershire, Rod Bransgrove at

Hampshire, Jamie Clifford at Kent, Jim Cumbes at Lancashire, Neil Davidson and David Smith at Leicestershire, Vinny Codrington at Middlesex, Mark Tagg at Northamptonshire, Derek Brewer at Nottinghamshire, Richard Gould and Andy Nash at Somerset, Paul Sheldon at Surrey, Dave Brooks at Sussex, Colin Povey at Warwickshire, Mark Newton at Worcestershire, Stewart Regan at Yorkshire and Angus Porter at the Professional Cricketers' Association. In addition Matthew Fleming, Tim Lamb, Andrew Renshaw, David Warner and Nigel Williamson provided helpful insights, as unwittingly did county members and members of the public at different grounds around the country.

My thanks go also to my editor at A&C Black, Charlotte Atyeo, for commissioning and encouraging a book that changed direction once or twice, and especially to Paul Millman without whose help none of this would have come together in the time available. In between his commitments to Sport England and England Squash, notably chairing the selection of six Delhi Commonwealth Games medallists, he arranged all my interviews with his former county colleagues, travelled the country with me, helped analyse the conversations and read the manuscript at different stages. We had worked briefly on a project some years ago, nothing to do with cricket, and his renewed friendship was part of the enjoyment in writing on a subject, county cricket, which we both feel deserves more recognition and support than it receives.

To that supposedly dying band of supporters, the county members, who live on from season to season, wanting nothing more than company, conversation and a County Championship title.

CHAPTER ONE
SWANSEA WITH THE RAGTOP DOWN

Some years ago I spent my summer Saturdays covering county cricket for the *Independent on Sunday*. Early morning starts, late nights home, avoiding motorways when I could, criss-crossing country roads with the ragtop down. Dylan, Springsteen and Van Morrison on the tape deck. One season I tried to work a Dylan or a Springsteen reference into every match report; something to amuse the subs. Driving home, the listening would also be Radio 3, and by the Last Night of the Proms the hood was usually up, the nights were getting cold and the summer was almost done. They were good days.

Even when the cricket wasn't memorable, and too many times it wasn't, the company always was. Sport, and not just cricket, has that effect on writers whose ambitions don't stretch to far-off horizons. A well-drawn pint, the fug from freeloaded Benson & Hedges, good gossip and the opportunity to bitch about a more-favoured colleague could transform a mediocre day's cricket into 500 enthusiastic words by the close of play. Back then anyway. They banned smoking in the press box, I seem to think, and looking at the papers now I get the impression they're trying to do away with cricket writing from the county grounds. All of which is beginning to make me sound like a grumpy old man. I've no reason to be. I know how lucky I was, and others before me were even luckier.

Covering cricket matches took me all around England. Wales, too, once I realised that the road to Gwasanaethau wouldn't get me further than a Little Chef or a BP pump. Out-grounds usually drew a good crowd and some interesting characters but, never one for camping, I preferred the solidity of a press box to a tent tucked away at long leg or deep mid-off. The ranks of empty seats at the county grounds, especially the Test match grounds, never bothered me much because my focus of interest was the cricket and the cricketers. When I did once write that there were more men carrying shopping home from Sainsbury's than there were in a certain county ground, a senior cricket correspondent wigged me next day for giving the game away. 'Once sports editors believe that no one's watching, they'll stop giving space to county cricket,' was the gist of the message. He had a point.

Even so you did have to wonder how county cricket kept going, especially the County Championship, when so few people watched it. There was always the county membership, mostly in the background but out in numbers for the big one-day games. And there was the money channelled down to the counties by the Test and County Cricket Board (TCCB) from international matches, television and sponsorship. The subsidy, some called it, while others, less charitable, deemed it a handout. Whatever it was, it was a lifeline, and county cricket stumbled from season to season attached to it. The day of reckoning was always around another corner.

What got my goat was the fact that, with so much county cricket, England too often struggled to produce a decent national side. A half-decent one would have sufficed sometimes. Quite why I got all hot under the collar about it is another matter altogether. It's not as if England was my country, and as the *Daily Telegraph* once told its readers, I didn't even pass the Tebbit Test – the theory, propounded by former Conservative MP Norman Tebbit, that their allegiance at cricket determined whether members of ethnic minorities were truly British. I supported the country of my birth, New Zealand, and let's face it there were years either side of Richard Hadlee when New Zealand cricket needed all the support it could get.

So what was I doing, arguing for a reduction in the number of English first-class counties, flying kites about city cricket, writing in *Wisden Cricketers' Almanack* that the county system got by on a confederacy of mediocrity? These were decent, hard-working people I was castigating, as a few of them reminded me, and maybe that was part of the problem. They were too nice to bring on the reforms I considered necessary if England weren't to be rolled over every time they took the field against Australia. Not that I wasn't keeping good company. In his 2008 book, *Pommies*, William Buckland brackets me with Bob Willis, Mike Atherton and Ian Chappell as one of 'the usual suspects' when it came to blaming county cricket and the game's administration for England's on-field ills. True, Ian Chappell and I didn't open the bowling or batting for England; nor did we captain England. But what the hell, you can't win them all.

I guess the answer is that I enjoy cricket as a game. I've never been sentimental about it, but as a critic I always believed, and still do, that it deserves more than 22 players simply going through the motions. And I did sometimes think that this was all I was watching. Not always, of course. There was an afternoon at Southampton – pre-Rose Bowl at cosy, comfortable, tumbledown Northlands Road – when I thought I'd stroll around the ground before sending over my early-edition copy. Halfway round, Hampshire's 35-year-old left-arm seamer, Kevan James, dismissed Vikram Rathore, Sachin Tendulkar, Rahul Dravid and Sanjay Manjrekhar in the space of four balls, precipitating not just an Indian collapse but also a hasty rewrite. Next day James hit a hundred to complete a unique double. Then there was a day in Swansea, not a writing day, when a couple of balls from a young Welsh quick were fast enough to stop you talking in mid-sentence and wonder if you should believe what you'd seen. He was all over the place, it's true, and for two years running *Wisden* mentioned that this raw pace needed 'harnessing'. But he was just out of his teens and some good judges, among them Glamorgan's soon-to-be-England-coach, Duncan Fletcher, thought Simon Jones a likely lad to watch. It took a few years, but in 2005 his name was on everyone's lips, male or female, whatever the reason.

Hampshire chairman Rod Bransgrove, the pharmaceuticals businessman whose personal millions and entrepreneurial drive bankrolled the Rose Bowl dream, also looks back with affection on his days watching cricket at Northlands Road, not from the privileged sanctum of the committee room but out with the punters, enjoying a few beers and a Zantac burger, 'so called because it was guaranteed to give you indigestion. I enjoyed all that about cricket, that was the charm of the game.' Northlands Road and Zantac burgers are a far cry from the albatross he took on when Hampshire faced bankruptcy at the beginning of the new century.

Nor is the Rose Bowl, a state-of-the-architect stadium built on farmland on the outskirts of Southampton, the sole albatross around the neck of a county cricket club chairman. Within a year of England regaining the Ashes in 2009, the game was awash with the cries of albatrosses coming home to roost. To mix an avian metaphor with a mammoth cliché, it was the year when stadiums became the white elephant in cricket's committee rooms. The trouble with elephants, however, is that they're great, hefty beasts; they hide more than the cracks that have been papered over for decades. They obscure the bigger picture as well as the small one.

It's not something unique to cricket. Other professional sports have had to go through intense and painful years of transition, struggling to determine where they should be as both sports and sporting businesses, to decide whether they are sports within a business or a business within sport. English football went through it with the development of the Premier League, creating not just a new domestic competition but also an international brand. On a smaller scale, perhaps more appropriate to cricket's situation, rugby union took a long look at itself and emerged anew with its own club Premiership.

'Rugby had quite a painful transition,' said Colin Povey, chief executive of Warwickshire County Cricket Club since 2006 and for some ten years a non-executive director at Northampton Saints rugby club, 'and some of the things we recognise in cricket are still prevalent in rugby. But the standard of club rugby is exceptionally high, so it's a fantastic product. The other thing rugby has done right is that the game has invested in facilities, so the stadiums by and large are excellent. They give fans a really good experience alongside a good product, and unfortunately that's not something that can yet be said about cricket in a consistent fashion.'

Not if you're a fan, that's for sure. And don't even think about the experience once you're inside the ground. Give some thought to what you might see when you get there. In fact, let's be off-the-wall about this and go back to Bruce Springsteen, not so much to The Boss himself but to his E Street Band sidekick, Steve Van Zandt, or Miami Steve from Southside Johnny and the Asbury Jukes, or Little Steven and the Disciples of Soul, or Silvio Dante of *The Sopranos*. We're not, incidentally, talking here of the Steve Van Zandt who co-hosted a morning radio show on WROW coming out of Albany, New York, but the syndicated radio host of 'Little Steven's Underground Garage'.

Struggling to keep up at the back? Then spare a thought for the hapless cricket supporter as he tries to work his way around the domestic fixture maze, assuming he's not lost somewhere in the international house of cards. There's the FPt20, which used to be the T20 Cup and was the Twenty20 Cup when the competition kicked off in 2003 (FP incidentally was once the 50-overs sponsor); there's the CB40, not connected to UB40 but with county grounds stag-ing concerts you can never be sure; and somewhere, here there and everywhere, there's the poor old County Championship, supposedly the one they all want to win, if they're not too busy trying to avoid relegation, the one with integrity according to the ECB. On top of which there are all the England teams' international games, be they Test matches over five days (or fewer), 50 overs or 20 overs. You pay your money and you take your pick. It's all cricket apparently, rather like Wittgenstein's duck and his rabbit or the many faces of Steve Van Zandt. You can't see more than one version at one and the same time, that's all.

Or maybe you don't take your pick or pay your money, and after a while you stop bothering too much about cricket. It isn't hard to do, especially if you don't have a Sky subscription and so have no access to televised cricket. You still follow the game in the papers, of course, but over the years the coverage of county cricket has fallen away alarmingly. Premiership club rugby gets three, sometimes four times the coverage that county cricket gets. I've been counting the column inches. The papers are all about England, which is fair enough because, by and large, Team England in their tripartite manifestations are doing all right. But what about the counties? They're still the game's lifeblood, developing and providing the international players, and more than that they have held the key to the romance of cricket, its literature, its history and its place in the rhythms of the English summer. I've never had a lot of time for St Paul; he strikes me as more confusing than the fixture list. But if there was ever a time for a 'usual suspect' to have a Damascene moment, I reckon that time is now.

Several of the counties, especially those with international grounds, are saddled with debt, while attendances at Test matches have been falling away alarmingly. There is talk of over-capacity. The extended midsummer Twenty20 competition in 2010 was so flat for many counties that the structure of the domestic programme came under fire yet again and under pressure for another revamp. There was talk of breakaways and muttering about Indian Premier League-style franchises. The chairman of the ECB was threatened with a slander suit, and for a few days no one wanted Kevin Pietersen to play for them; not England, not the counties, certainly not his own county, Hampshire. Some insiders were even suggesting that the business of county cricket was unsustainable – nothing new there – and ready to implode. County cricket needed a champion.

CHAPTER TWO

BUSINESS FIRST, CRICKET SECOND?

Tim Lamb, chief executive of the TCCB in 1996, and of its successor the ECB from 1997 to 2004, said when appointed that he believed cricket should be 'a business within a game, not a game within a business'. Had cricket sustained that distinction? I asked him in early 2010 at the offices of the Central Council of Physical Recreation (now renamed the Sport and Recreation Alliance), where he had been chief executive since 2005.

'I'd like to think it still applies,' he answered. 'It should apply, because cricket, football, rugby and similar activities, they are principally sports. But they do have to be run along businesslike lines.'

Nothing wrong with that, except that people who are good at business have been notorious over the years for leaving their business brains at the door of sports club boardrooms and committee rooms. 'The Average Director's Knowledge of Football', the often-quoted chapter in Len Shackleton's 1956 autobiography *Clown Prince of Soccer*, didn't become one of the most eloquent blank pages in sports writing for nothing. As we try to get to grips with the way county cricket operates, along with the difficulties in which some county clubs have found themselves, there might be a temptation to see that blank page as something of a recurring theme, albeit one with a few caveats.

An even greater temptation will be to lay blame on the ECB. But as Tim Lamb points out, it has to be remembered that the ECB is in essence an association of its members. And those members, says the ECB's constitution (it does have one), are the chairmen of the 18 first-class counties, the MCC chairman, the chairmen of the remaining

21 County Cricket Boards not in a first-class county and, provided he or she doesn't already feature among the aforementioned, the chairman of the Minor Counties Cricket Association. Oh sweet Dickie Bird, I feel a Van Zandt moment coming on, and I still haven't got my heart around the loss of Rutland.

'I always argued that the ECB was bigger than the sum of its parts,' Lamb said, but he couldn't ignore the reality that the counties could always elect another chairman if they didn't like what the ECB executives were doing, and the new chairman could always replace the executives. 'The first-class counties held the power; they had reserve powers such as approval of the budget and of the playing programme.'

The ECB was constituted to be the governing body for all aspects of cricket in England and Wales, from the national teams down to the grass roots: for the professional game, through the medium of the First-Class Forum, to the amateur game under the Recreational Forum. Initially the two forums elected four nominees each to the ECB's 14-man Management Board, but it wasn't long before the first-class counties' nominees were increased to five. There was never any doubt who would be the dog and who would wag the tail, and it was a pretty big hound from the sound of it. Too big maybe, if this anecdote of a First-Class Forum meeting is any reflection.

'There were as many as 45 to 50 people in the room, all the county chairmen and chief executives, plus various people from the ECB. The big topic of discussion was online rights, all exciting stuff, and in the middle of Mr Robert Griffiths QC banging on about them, Don Trangmar, the Sussex chairman, turned his chair round, got his newspaper out and, to everyone's amazement, started reading.'

Shades of Warwick 'The Big Ship' Armstrong who, while captaining Australia at The Oval in 1921, took himself off to the outfield and began reading a newspaper. Asked what he was reading, he said he was trying to discover who they were playing. Perhaps Mr Trangmar had a good knowledge of cricket history as well as sharing with Armstrong a low boredom threshold.

'The First-Class Forum got there in the end, but it was a tortuous process,' admitted former Essex wicketkeeper David East, now the county's chief executive. So it's maybe not surprising that the ECB decided there should be fewer meetings of the counties, with more power being invested in the Management Board. In 2005, less than ten years after it was set up, the First-Class Forum was quietly side-lined when the ECB replaced the burgeoning 18-man Management Board with a slimmer 12-man Board of Directors, including three from the first-class counties and two from the recreational game.

Tom Richardson, Gloucestershire's chief executive since 2001, thought that, 'in a funny sort of way, in a slightly gentlemanly way, the First-Class Forum did work. You wouldn't normally pick a committee that big to make decisions, but that's where we were. And if you look at what the First-Class Forum achieved, well it brought in Twenty20, academies and central contracts for a start. Little by little, though, the county chairmen started to change. We saw some much more business-oriented chairmen coming in and they were the cata-lyst. Clearly what we have now is more streamlined and maybe the First-Class Forum had had its day, but it would be wrong to dismiss it as unworkable.'

The Board of Directors, the 12 men good and true, increased to 14 in 2010 with the addition of two women: the ubiquitous Rachael Heyhoe-Flint as the women's game representative, and Jane Stichbury, former chief constable of Dorset and the first woman appointed to be an HM Inspector of Constabulary, as an independent director. I've never really rumbled what the board does. Administers, directs and manages the business and affairs of the ECB, perhaps. That's what boards of directors are supposed to do, though being on a board can also mean, 'Have another chocolate biscuit and don't talk with your mouth full'.

It's what the ECB board can't do that's interesting. It can't stop a first-class county from playing in the domestic competitions, and if it wants to flex its muscles with regard to first-class cricket it must talk to the counties first. This is commonly called consultation, and after tripping around the county grounds of England, talking to county chief executives and some chairmen, I was left with the impression that ECB-style consultation can come in any colour as long as it's black. Being a fair-minded fellow, I was inclined to think this viewpoint a little extreme, but partway through my travels an ECB consultation document dropped on the desks of the 18 chief execs, outlining five options to restructure the County Championship. It went out towards the end of April; replies were to be in by 4 July, a funny date to choose given the reaction across the Pond to bossy-boots governance emanating from London. But then a later date, say 5 November, would have been no less incendiary.

The five options on the tablet were:

- A Premier division of eight counties playing each other home and away; a secondary division split into north and south pools with counties playing those in their own pool twice and those in the other pool once.
- Three conferences, presumably of six counties apiece, with play-offs.
- Three divisions of six counties with matches played over five days.
- Two divisions of nine counties playing 12 to 14 matches.
- Three divisions of seven comprising the current counties and three minor counties, with promotion and relegation of one county per division.

You get the feeling that someone at the ECB really was listening to Steve Van Zandt.

'That paper was disappointing,' said Leicestershire's David Smith when I saw him in mid-May. 'For me there are two things on there that are red herrings: five-day Championship cricket and 21 counties. I'm not sure who David [ECB chief executive David Collier] consulted with, or did he do it on his own? He's supposed to have a cricket committee and they're supposed to be empowered to make recommendations. I'm not saying he didn't consult anyone, but there was nothing formally requested from the group.'

At Old Trafford Jim Cumbes was no less dismissive. 'I think the ECB have an idea, and then they talk about consulting with everybody. But it's only "consult" because that's what they say they're going to do. The structure that's been put out about the Championship, five-day cricket, 12 games, 14 games, there's been no discussion about it at all, no discussion with the cricket committee and they should have been consulted. Everybody has looked at it and said, "I don't like any of that," because there's been no input from the counties.'

And why just the County Championship? As Rod Bransgrove says, 'You should never be reviewing just one competition in isolation. We should be looking at the English cricket season as a whole. When I receive questionnaires from the ECB, I sometimes wonder whether the answers have already been ticked. For me, sending out a multiple-choice questionnaire is not an ideal process of consultation. It's never audited and we never really know how people answered.'

Or as former Kent chief executive Paul Millman put it, 'Fill in a form and we'll let you know what the outcome is.'

I'd known Paul from before he was at Kent (1999–2009), back when he was managing director of Merrydown Wine, the Sussex-based cider-maker whose company history I wrote. For a time Merrydown was Sussex County Cricket Club's sponsor, and the more I got into researching this book the more I noticed similarities between county cricket and Merrydown's early years. Something was always coming along 'to bring home the bacon' as co-founder Ian Howie used to say. First there was the 65-over knockout competition, which quickly became the 60-over Gillette Cup; next came the 40-over John Player Sunday League and very soon the 50-over Benson & Hedges Cup. More recently, after interest in these was waning, up popped Twenty20, cricket's answer to the Aussie alcopop, Two Dogs, which for several months had Merrydown's share price soaring. Nor should we overlook the commercial cash cows of sponsorship and broadcasting rights.

An England squash international for the best part of ten years and later chairman of selectors, Paul also kept wicket for Gloucestershire seconds in the 1960s; a distant relative, Geoff Millman, kept wicket for England and Nottinghamshire in the 1950s and 1960s, as well as captaining Notts from 1963 to 1965. For some reason, during his time as chief exec at Canterbury, Paul had taken exception to my comment in *Wisden* that county cricket was a Victorian institution that had resisted reform in the 20th century and was struggling into the 21st on subsidies rather than public support. We crossed words a few times. But for all that, he was one of the first people I approached when I started to look further into the business of county cricket. Apart from anything else, he was one of the few I still knew in cricket administration.

It wasn't only the people who had changed. Titles and executive responsibilities were different as well. A glance at the 1990 *Wisden Almanack* shows 11 first-class county secretaries, two secretary/managers and five chief executives, with Kent employing both a secretary and a chief executive to confuse the arithmetic. Another 20 years on and the only secretaries in sight were at Lord's, where MCC and Middlesex compromised with secretary/chief executive for the men in charge of the clubs' day-to-day operations.

But then, what's in a name? It's only a title, except that with the change in title had also come a change in mindset, a perceptive shift away from the secretary being a servant of the committee and county members. Not that the members always acknowledged this. The new breed of chief executives usually came from management backgrounds with years of business experience on their CVs and they understood big boys' rules: the line you walk, the bottom line, is a fine one, and you stand or fall by the success of the business, not necessarily by Championship positions or Twenty20 finals. Recycling management, rather like setting up royal commissions or root and branch reviews, gives people the impression that something is being done. It might not solve the problems – as often as not, it doesn't – but it does buy time for the chairman of the board – or in cricket's case, of the committee.

Tim Lamb sympathises with his previous colleagues, many of whom he still meets up with at Lord's on the occasion of their annual chief executives' dinner. 'When you're in the thick of a job, living it 24 hours a day with issues coming in from all directions, you have to step back sometimes and look at yourself and your priorities. You're often so busy dealing with the day-to-day fire-fighting that the strategic thinking gets lost.'

Jamie Clifford, who succeeded Paul Millman at Kent, having previously been the county's director of business development, discovered early on that the chief executive's role is a lot different when you're in it from when you're observing it. 'I have a completely different perspective on the demands now,' he laughed. 'Bearing in mind a county club is a relatively small business, you need to have an awareness of every aspect of what's going on, whether it's the person cutting the grass or running the finances. As chief exec you have a responsibility for all the people in your organisation, and the fact that they all come to you when they've got an issue or a problem, well that goes with the territory. The fact that there are other senior managers doesn't isolate you from the expectations of the other people in the business. They look to you to lead.'

'Everybody I spoke to when I was working in the game said how difficult this is as a business,' Millman added. 'People on the outside don't always believe just how difficult it is until they actually get involved. That applies to chairmen as well as chief executives.'

Around the county grounds, inevitably, there are still murmurers muttering into their thermos-flask tea and homemade ham sandwiches that the new-style administrators don't come with a cricketing pedigree, as for example Lamb himself did: Oxford University, Middlesex and Northamptonshire. In 2010 only three of the county bosses had played first-class cricket, and that went down to two at the end of June when David Smith, former Warwickshire opening batsman, son of a former Leicestershire professional and brother of Warwickshire all-rounder Paul, resigned as Leicestershire chief executive. Interference in team selection by chairman Neil Davidson and other board members was said to be the reason, a claim Davidson rejected, and in a summer not devoid of controversies and damaging headlines the matter rumbled on until Davidson, too, stepped down.

Of the remaining two, Essex's David East had kept wicket for the county in the 1980s. At Taunton in 1985, on his 26th birthday, he equalled Wally Grout's then world record of eight catches in an innings; that they were the first eight Somerset wickets made it a unique achievement. Jim Cumbes, the Lancashire chief executive, had bowled a lively fast-medium for Lancashire, Surrey, Worcestershire and Warwickshire over a 20-year stretch, while in an equally peripatetic soccer career he played in goal for Tranmere Rovers, West Bromwich Albion, Aston Villa and Worcester City. There's nothing on record to say if he worked for Tony Soprano.

It's not only the members, and some in the media come to that, who are critical of the fact that not enough former county cricketers are involved in running the game. Hugh Morris, Mike Gatting, John Carr, Phil Neale, Steve Elworthy and Alan Fordham are former first-class cricketers holding down management positions at the ECB, but, David Smith wondered, where else but in sport would a board of directors contain only two people with hands-on experience of the core product. Such was the case with the 14-strong ECB board, on which only Warwickshire's Dennis Amiss and Kent's Matthew Fleming had played (men's) international and county cricket.

'I'm not suggesting for one moment that it should be full of ex-players,' Smith said, 'because it shouldn't be. You need a variety of rounded skills. But it's not unreasonable to think that four out of the 14 would have played first-class cricket and would be there to direct the business people around some of the challenges they've got.

We haven't got that; we've got two. The number's wrong. The ECB should have ensured they had a board that is reflective of their core product and reflects the commercial needs to meet the challenges the game now faces.'

But how essential is first-class cricket experience when it comes to the day-to-day administration of a county? These days most counties have a director of cricket or cricket manager who takes charge of the playing side, although perhaps it's pertinent that Leicestershire didn't have one when their laundry appeared in public. Former player Tim Boon's designated role was senior coach, a somewhat old-fashioned title more in keeping with the traditional county structure in which the members' committee thought it pulled the strings.

Dave Brooks, Sussex's good-natured chief executive, sees the way that the coach's role has developed as indicative of the way cricket itself has evolved from a sport to a business. 'It wasn't really all that many years ago that some of the counties didn't even have a coach. The captain and the cricket committee were left to get on with it. Today the coach's role has become much more sophisticated. Instead of there being just the one coach in a county, there's a whole support team now and the director of cricket role has evolved. Consequently the chief executive has required less knowledge of cricket and has become much more business focused. Obviously an appreciation helps, but you don't need to be quite as involved as was the case historically.'

Before joining Sussex in 2009, Brooks was chief executive of Finsbury Food Group, an AIM-listed bakery business, 'with a £200 million turnover employing 3,000 people. In many respects it was a different industry, but in other respects it's the same. You're still trying to provide people with something they enjoy at good value. Instead of it being a chocolate cake it's a game of cricket.'

During his job interview, he admits, he did get the impression that the club thought it would be 'quite a punt' to appoint a chief executive from a non-cricketing background. The man he was replacing, Gus Mackay, had played one-day international cricket for Zimbabwe before moving into cricket administration in England. But Mackay was going to The Oval to fill the newly created post of managing director of cricket for Surrey, a make-of-it-what-you-will title at a county which in 2009 could also boast a professional cricket manager, a coach/consultant, batting and bowling coaches and a chairman of cricket – as well as, by the end of the season, third from bottom in the Championship second division, bottom of the Pro40 second division and nothing to write home about in the 50-over and Twenty20 competitions. As Sussex won both the Pro40 and Twenty20 and were finalists of the 50-over in his first season, Brooks might have been justified in thinking a cricketing background a tad over-rated, even if Sussex were relegated in the Championship. To everyone's joy at Hove they jumped straight back in 2010, whereas Surrey remained down among the dead men in division two and Mackay was among the casualties when Surrey began cutting back staff with a ruthlessness not always seen on the field.

If Sussex had thought they might be taking a punt on Brooks, he himself initially wondered what value his plc experience would be to them. 'I said this right at the start, and it's still valid today. Because of its private members and the culture of the business, Sussex County Cricket Club has more in common with my local village club than it has with Finsbury Food Group.'

What Brooks and his fellow chief executives do, in effect, is run a management team. A comparison of administrative staff with playing staff soon puts the business of county cricket into an unexpected perspective. Doing this exercise a few years ago, I reckoned it averaged out at two and a half non-playing staff for every cricketer. Only Middlesex had more cricketers than non-playing staff. Yet Surrey, no surprise there, were the one county where admin salaries exceeded the cricketers' wages. By way of a more recent example, the Essex playing staff for the 2009 season – 23 – accounted for 21 per cent of the overall staff. At Nottinghamshire, the cricket staff (24) made up

31 per cent of the Trent Bridge employees. Of the 182 employed at Old Trafford, only 26 were on the playing and coaching side, whereas Northamptonshire had 25 admin people compared with 27 players and 19 coaching staff. Kent were more slimline, with their 21 cricketers representing almost a third of their staff under contract.

If any chief executive might be expected to put cricket before business, it would be a former player. But David East, having probably spent more time of late in meetings with planners, lawyers, developers and the local authorities than in watching cricket, has no doubt where the priorities lie. 'We chief executives run the operational side of the business; we're at the coalface of the business and understand that side of it. We see ourselves, me and my colleagues around the country, as guardians of the game in our county while we're involved with it. We'd like to see the county we're working for – in my case the county I have a passion for – being in a better place than when we joined.'

There's a touch of Edmund Burke in this. Of inheriting the legacy of the previous generation and passing it on to the next; the partnership between those who are dead, those who are living and those who are yet to be born. Our role is to be stewards, John Woodcock told me when I succeeded him as editor of *Wisden*, to preserve what's gone before. It's an ethic, a belief even, that was evident in East's commitment both to Essex and to county cricket.

'I think in this job you have to like the game, but it's business first, cricket second,' agreed Derek Brewer, who became Nottinghamshire's chief executive in 2005 after David Collier left Trent Bridge to head up the ECB executive at Lord's. And in case anyone's thinking that this is the philosophy of a non-cricketing administrator, Brewer represented British Universities and had half a season with Warwickshire seconds in the days when he was 'a tall, gangly off-spinner'. Edgbaston teammates included David Smith's younger brother, Tony, and future England internationals Eddie Hemmings and 18-year-old Kim Barnett.

Brewer's career, however, lay elsewhere, and his cricket was played mostly in various leagues as he moved around the country and up the banking ladder. Nottinghamshire recruited him for his experience in corporate lending, human resources and performance management – as a regional director with the Royal Bank of Scotland he'd been responsible for teams of 200 to 300. These were the skills, not his off-break bowling, that Trent Bridge needed. Even so, the fact that Notts were county champions twice and runners-up twice in his first six years will remain highlights of his time at Trent Bridge. Because, business first or cricket first, the cricket is always important when you're running a cricket club.

Down in Taunton, Richard Gould had no hesitation in stating the game's pre-eminence. 'Our aim is to play cricket to the highest possible level. We want people around us in Somerset to be enthused by our success and so play more cricket. There are some grounds where you hear the senior officers saying their objective is to be an international venue. Well, as soon as you concentrate on that, what happens to the domestic thing you're doing? Our mission statement says it's our ambition to win trophies and compete consistently in all formats of domestic cricket in order to promote Somerset and England throughout the cricket world. Full stop.'

For all Gould's conviction about the game's pre-eminence in the Somerset cricket business, his background is not cricket. He'd been an officer in the Royal Tank Regiment before moving into sports admin-istration as commercial director at Bristol City Football Club. Nothing surprising in that career move. His father, Bobby Gould, had banged in goals for more clubs than Jim Cumbes had hot dinners, among them Coventry City, Arsenal, Wolves, West Brom, both Bristols and Hereford United; as a manager he took Wimbledon to Wembley and a famous FA Cup final win over Liverpool in 1988. Richard's goalkeeper brother, Jonathan, played league football in England and Scotland before becoming a coach in New Zealand. Somerset paid for Richard to take Harvard Business School's advanced management course – an act that illustrates how keen the club are to ensure they continually improve what they do, both in the present and looking ahead.

'It's all about creating, about delivering, the best service for our sport and our members,' he acknowledged. 'Some people might say that sounds like crass marketing talk, but in fact it's very important. Look at how rugby has gained in popularity. In part that's due to the improvement in their facilities, so that when you go to a game it's easy to get into the ground, you've got a nice place to sit, you've got good sightlines. You look at football, which benefited from the safety reports into the game 15 or so years ago. The clubs increased the culture of the facilities, and their crowds grew at exactly the same time.'

The irony is that the culture of the facilities is why some counties found themselves in such a dilemma by 2010. Courting that culture had meant embracing another culture, the culture of borrowing and debt, which had cast uncertainty not only over cricket, not only over other major sports, but also over commerce, education, governments, families, individuals, all walks of life. Cricket was simply another social construct coming to terms with the day of reckoning. The question it had to answer was whether or not the county clubs could work collectively for the good of all, to create a common structure for the future of professional cricket in England and Wales. Or was it a case that the game would remain in conflict, on and off the field, as 18 different, often disparate, businesses?

CHAPTER THREE

GOING DOWN TO THE CROSSROADS

The gloom-mongers were out hawking their scares early doors in 2010. And with the English cricket season starting in Abu Dhabi on 29 March – the first home game was on 3 April – the doors were indeed opening early on the drama that would play out around the counties in the months ahead. Not the on-field dramas, of which there was no shortage once Pakistan's itinerant team pitched up in England, but the dramatic developments in which the very existence of some clubs was questioned. As the counties began reporting and accounting in keeping with their variable year endings, the media soon latched on to the six-figure losses announced by almost half of them. Quite why the morbid interest is a matter of conjecture, for there was nothing new in the first-class counties coming out with annual deficits. They have always been something of a perennial. Perhaps it was another example of the new broom of economic puritanism that was sweeping the land in the aftermath of the financial crisis.

Kent took the dubious pride of place with their headline-grabbing pre-tax deficit of £811,952 – a bitter blow, coming on top of the previous year's loss of £706,536 – while at the other end of the scale Warwickshire were the good news Bears with a record pre-tax profit of £1.15 million. Surrey (£752,000) and Yorkshire (£698,826) similarly recorded record profits, but they also sent shivers down the backbone by revealing that they had paid out £1.7 million and £790,000 respectively in annual interest and bank charges. While not having access to all the figures, and using my idiosyncratic back-of-an-envelope accounting methods, I reckon something around

£2 million net, more than £3 million gross, went out of the game in interest and charges in the 2009 reporting year.

HOW THE COUNTIES STOOD IN 2009

	PROFIT/(LOSS)	CURRENT ASSETS	LIABILITIES DUE in 1 yr	LIABILITIES DUE more than 1 yr
	£	£	£	£
Derbyshire[4]	14,420	1,356,118	376,412	—
Durham[1]	145,859	4,322,436	3,810,852	3,915,679
Essex[4]	(244,789)	1,049,785	1,256,949	94,696
Glamorgan[4]	338,324	686,334	2,274,663	12,188,401
Gloucestershire[1]	(182,000)	1,018,000	1,316,000	682,000
Hampshire[2]	(532,000)	1,401,000	15,712,000	4,093,000
Kent[2]	(811,952)	906,720	3,202,969	1,036,133
Lancashire[4]	(605,099)	1,891,039	3,765,583	9,227,850
Leicestershire[1]	689	612,316	333,043	206,871
Middlesex[4]	(114,000)	3,674,000	818,000	—
Northamptonshire[1]	2,945	1,300,790	1,279,585	767,712
Nottinghamshire[1]	(148,761)	2,368,454	3,609,664	13,989,253
Somerset[1]	6,357	1,426,844	1,703,932	1,237,038
Surrey[3]	752,000	7,217,000	10,474,000	23,435,000
Sussex[2]	(15,729)	11,490,207	1,781,809	—
Warwickshire[1]	1,156,396	4,804,596	6,376,474	2,270,840
Worcestershire[1]	(118,439)	509,466	1,720,517	2,577,492
Yorkshire[4]	698,826	413,391	4,650,158	16,874,612

[1] Year ending 30.9.2009   [2] Year ending 31.10.2009
[3] Year ending 30.11.2009   [4] Year ending 31.12.2009

NOTE: The above figures have been extracted mostly from county Report and Accounts. The variation in accounting methods means that it is not possible to produce like-for-like figures.

So now, in addition to annual losses, commentators and headline writers fixed their attention on the levels of debt that counties, the Test match counties in particular, had taken on in order to finance ground and facilities improvements so as to comply with the ECB's Technical Specification for Facilities (TSF1 from 1998 to 2006, and subsequently TSF2). Was there a similar level of fascination in the substantial increase in interest payments made by the counties back in 2005, also as a result of heavy borrowing to fund stadium improvements? Probably not. In 2005 the prevailing mood was euphoria forever rather than apocalypse now. England had regained the Ashes at long last, and throughout the country cricket was good news again. Who needed then to be told that £2 million or more were going out of the game in interest payments?

Not even the usual suspects were talking of counties going to the wall in 2005. But they were five years later; it was back to gloom and doom as usual. It was almost reassuring, come to think of it, because the specious nature of county cricket has always meant that one county or another has been under threat some time or another. History, however, suggests it's something of a hollow threat. Does anyone really believe that one of the 18 counties will be allowed to go down river?

'You can't let grounds go bust, even if in reality that's what should happen,' said Sussex's Dave Brooks with the assurance of someone whose own county's finances had been underwritten by a £12 million legacy from a former president, Spen Cama. And over at Essex, David East is a strong believer in having 18 counties. 'It's a good structure for us. For as long as I can remember we've been arguing about the sustainability and viability of all the counties. One or two have got into some fairly desperate straits before and we're all still here.'

Indeed, Darwinists might despair at the way cricket's weak have managed to co-exist with the strong, with their survival in the hands of a higher authority. But then, as Professor David Papineau noted in reviewing *What Darwin Got Wrong*, by Jerry Fodor and Massimo

Piattelli-Palmarini, 'Natural selection can only tinker with pre-existing designs, and so is often stuck with historical hangovers... natural selection is often constrained by the materials it is given to work with.'

Put forward the proposal that 18 first-class counties are too many and the average reply is, 'You wouldn't choose to have 18 if you were starting afresh, but 18 is what we have and we have to manage as best we can.' Yet it wasn't so very long ago that there were 17 first-class counties and some of us claimed that 17 were too many. The Darwinians around the Long Room at Lord's, and doubtless some dogma-dancing Friedmanites, should have been agreeing with us that if counties continued to lose members, failed to attract bigger gates, fielded poor-quality teams and existed essentially on subsidies and benefits, then natural selection and the market should take their course. The weakest counties should go out of business. Leave the first-class lake and find a new life in the minor counties pond.

So what did cricket, this most unnatural of games, do? Instead of downsizing it evolved upwards by elevating Durham to the top tier, with effect from October 1991. More pertinently, in view of the current debt dilemma, Durham's promotion was subject to their having planning permission and funding for a new headquarters ground at Chester-le-Street, which would bring international cricket to the north-east. They were also told they had to raise a million pounds.

'At the time I think the club had £15,000 in the bank,' recollected David Harker, who joined Durham in 1991. 'I was one of five full-time employees: the chief exec, the groundsman, Geoff Cook as director of cricket, a secretary and me as financial controller.' He became chief executive in 2000, by which time the new Riverside ground at Chester-le-Street was operational, if by no means complete. It had already staged its first one-day international, in 1999, and the ground development was still a work in progress when Test cricket first came here in 2003.

'People don't necessarily appreciate that the reason we are staging international cricket is because it was required of us, rather than a means of jumping on the gravy train,' Harker said.

In fact, listening to old Durham hands talk, you begin to wonder just how much the TCCB wanted Durham's application for first-class status to go forward. It might have been thought a nice idea, a romantic one even in the way cricket does romance, but in setting their criteria the game's authorities might also have been hoping that they wouldn't be fulfilled. Crossing their fingers that the possibility of an 18th county would quietly disappear. It didn't work out that way.

'We were fortunate,' Harker pointed out, 'and unfortunate in another way, that European grant money was available at the time, so the club grew rapidly in terms of its capital infrastructure in the stadium. But it didn't grow quickly in terms of being able to generate revenue.'

Members were upset when a health club was built on the ground by a private developer prior to the Riverside's first Test match. But while the health club wasn't part of the original plan, it did help pay for 2,000 more permanent seats. And apart from voicing their objections, there wasn't a great deal the members could do about it because Durham was not strictly a members club. It may have felt and looked like one, but in becoming a first-class county Durham had registered as a company limited by guarantee, in effect a private company rather than a club. In time the business would bring in new directors and seek investment through shareholders rather than rely on borrowing. As Harker admits, this shift towards equity investment was essential if Durham were to progress not just as a venue but as a team.

'The motivation behind raising capital was to develop the stadium, but as a cricket club why have a stadium without a credible playing side? We took on £2 million of debt just to get the thing started, along with £3 million to £5 million worth of grant. We now have the overheads of a reasonably large stadium and we're not getting the income we need because we're not getting the international games. We can't borrow any more, we can't get the grants we originally had, so the only route left is equity investment.'

Even so it came as a surprise to many when in 2010 it was learnt that the equity investment, a very useful £2.4 million, had come from an Indian businessman, described by the club as 'a long-time friend and colleague of chairman Clive Leach'. There were grumblings about football clubs and foreign ownership, as if half the country wasn't in foreign or multinational ownership. The investment represented approximately 87 per cent of the club's shares currently in issue, so members logging on to the Durham website forum had every justification for expressing their concerns, along with some occasional indignation. My Merrydown book researches were a lesson in what can happen when businesses sell off shares of the company to raise capital. Over time the owners lose control of the business to the shareholders, and with shares being traded there's no knowing who those shareholders might be eventually.

'It was a means to an end to help us develop the stadium,' Harker reiterates. 'When we started there was a future in international cricket because the Riverside predates the Hampshire, Cardiff and Bristol grounds. I signed a three-year staging agreement [for international matches] on the understanding that the ECB wouldn't give any more staging agreements at the time. Within a year they'd given Yorkshire a 15-year agreement.'

Not without reason. There has been no shortage of people pointing a finger at Yorkshire, criticising their level of borrowing and the financial position they are in. But what was the club supposed to do? The alternative was not hosting Test cricket, and Yorkshire without Test cricket would have been anathema, not just for the county but also for cricket lovers and traditionalists everywhere. They had little option but to take the road they did, even if at every corner the devil of debt threatened to lead them by the hand into insolvency. Without the personal intervention of their chairman, Colin Graves, chairman of the Costcutter Supermarkets Group, they might not be in the business of playing even county cricket.

Yorkshire's 2009 accounts show that Graves and his family had lent the club £4.8 million. And that wasn't the half of it. He was also providing a shortfall guarantee on Leeds City Council's loan of £8.5 million secured against the ground itself, a £6.3 million guarantee in respect of HSBC Bank loans and overdrafts in the region of £4.5 million, and cash-flow support as required. On top of which Costcutter were one of Yorkshire's five official partners. What some of us still call sponsors.

After tax, Yorkshire's record profits dipped below £600,000, which wasn't going to make much of a dent in their immediate net debt of £4.2 million. Not that they were in a unique position for a business in 2009. With Britain coming out of recession, depending on whom you read or listen to, there was nothing out of the ordinary in Yorkshire having to roll debt over to the next year. Or the year after that. Debt soon becomes an ongoing business. Premier League football clubs' parlous finances and regular refinancing were everyday talking points in bars and boardrooms on both sides of the Atlantic, and emerging from behind the tut-tutting cricket headlines came news that Premier rugby club Wasps had reached an accommodation with the taxman over 'sizeable' unpaid taxes, having lost £2 million in the previous year.

Debt was the reality of professional sport in the 21st century. But as Derek Brewer spelled out, wearing his previous employment hat, this was nothing English cricket could be complacent about. 'In banking terms the sector is facing very high gearing levels.' In the absence of any mention of gearing in the MCC playing manual, Brewer apologised for the technical talk and explained that by gearing he was talking about borrowing levels in relation to a business's resources. 'Looking at our own situation we, like any other business, must ensure that our gearing is as low as possible and that we can service any debts we take on.'

Paul Millman thought some counties were finding it increasingly difficult to get going-concern status from their auditors, owing to the lack of security of their long-term cash flow. 'The auditors are saying, OK, you're a going concern. But strictly that's not always true. It's testing the interpretation of going concern.'

'Going concern' is the expression used by accountants and auditors to demonstrate that a business is in a financial position to continue trading for a certain period – a year is often the benchmark – without going into liquidation or being threatened with liquidation. It has to be able to realise its assets if necessary and pay whatever debts fall due in that time unless appropriate arrangements are in place: in Yorkshire's case, for example, assurances from a white-rose knight such as chairman Graves.

Paul had become my 'fixer', setting up meetings with the county chief executives and occasionally setting straight my years-old preconceptions and misconceptions about the way county cricket is run. Things had gone pear-shaped for the hop county in his last two years at Kent after the economic recession put their ambitious ground development plans on hold, so it was good to observe the warmth with which he was greeted by his former colleagues around the counties. It was as if they recognised that they all shared a common predicament – even while agreeing that the counties worked against each other off the field as much as on it. We'll come to that in due course.

Sometimes, too, the chief executives shared a common career background in the brewing industry, as was the case with Paul and the Yorkshire chief executive, Stewart Regan. Having worked his way up the ladder with John Smith, Stewart later held senior management positions at Bass; where as director of strategic planning he helped see through the takeover by American brewers Coors in 2002. The bonus he received for helping Bass achieve their price was the trigger he needed to change careers. 'I went from beer to football, which was something of a *Boy's Own* move really, and became managing director of the old First Division; what subsequently became the

Championship. Part of my brief was to redevelop the division into a much more customer-focused, aspirational brand. We brought in Coca Cola as sponsor and developed what became the Coca Cola Championship, which has operated as a vibrant second division below the Premier League.'

So when the headhunters came calling, hoping to lure him to Headingley as Yorkshire's chief executive, it didn't take him long to make his mind up. 'Knowing a little bit about the history of the club, I turned the job down. But around June 2005 I met Colin Graves, who was acting as chief executive, and he persuaded me that he had a vision to turn the club around. That relied on two key factors: getting a long staging arrangement from the ECB and buying the ground. The two things were connected, because if the ground wasn't purchased then the staging agreement fell away. Without the ground they couldn't do any of the necessary improvements.'

The ECB, through TSF1/2, required the Test match counties to have security of tenure of their grounds for at least 80 years, and suggested in addition that they should own them if possible. Should the ground ever be sold, any surplus or profit would have to go back into cricket.

'Colin was part of what we call the Gang of Four,' Regan continued. 'They were brought in when the bank threatened to pull the plug on the club in 2002. At that time the old committee had spent £5 million over budget on developing the East Stand at Headingley with no assets to underpin the debt. The bank allowed Colin and three other directors to come in and try to turn the club around: Geoff Cope, the former Yorkshire and England bowler, Robin Smith, who was then president of the club and a managing partner of the legal firm DLA Piper, and Brian Bouttell, a KPMG partner in the audit division. So lots of business experience there, and their first two years were spent trying to sort out the club's mess. They ended up stripping the cost base completely, parting company with a number of the staff, changing the constitution, getting rid of the old 23-man committee and putting in place a board with delegated powers to make decisions and run the club.'

'I don't suppose the members had any other choice,' Paul Millman observed. 'Otherwise the club would have gone under.'

'Correct,' Regan confirmed, 'the members had no choice. It was one of those turning points where through adversity the phoenix was reborn and the club was allowed to take off the shackles of the past and move forward. So the four directors spent two years preparing themselves to get the club into a healthier financial position and to put a business plan together. That business plan required the long staging agreement, because without it there was no way they could raise anything. They didn't own the ground, it was owned by Leeds rugby club next door, and they didn't own any income stream. There were no assets to raise capital against. The advertising, the catering, the pouring rights [brewery concession], they were all owned by the ground next door. The only asset they had was the club itself and the shirt sponsorship. That was really the only business they could do.

'So the club negotiated with the ECB and were successful in getting the last long-term staging agreement issued: 15 years from 2004 to 2019. Within that, though, there was the development plan that had to be delivered, and there was a poison-pill clause that said that if Yorkshire didn't purchase the Headingley ground by 31 December 2005, the staging agreement would fall away. That required a massive effort. Paul Caddick, the owner, was a tough negotiator and it took until 30 December to finally agree and to sign the contracts.'

There was more than these protracted negotiations to keep Yorkshire members on tenterhooks, however. Leeds City Council did not approve its £9 million prudential loan until 23 December, and it was Christmas Eve when members assembled for the special general meeting at which they voted overwhelmingly to allow the management board to purchase the ground. As local journalist David Warner wrote in *Wisden Almanack*, it was 'the first time ever that Yorkshire members in the same room had been unable to find something to argue about.'

'Prudential loans,' Regan explained, 'are effectively government money at a fixed interest rate, passed through central government down to the local authority in order to protect something of importance to the local region. Headingley cricket ground was seen as an essential item in the local economy, particularly having international cricket. So the club had the £9 million loan from prudential borrowing with £3 million of deferred payments to 2019 at the latest, and there was a £4.85 million option to buy out Paul Caddick's rights on the old Wintershed at the Kirkstall Lane end. In essence, then, it would cost £13 million to own the ground outright.

'So that was the position in 2005. I got a call on New Year's Eve to say that the deal had been done, and on 3 January 2006 I gave in my notice with the Football League. I joined Yorkshire on 1 March and at the AGM a fortnight later myself and Geoffrey Boycott were appointed to the board and Geoff Cope stood down. Including the appointed director from Leeds City Council we became a board of six, and the next two years were all about building the development plan, trying to think of how we could develop the stadium when we were already saddled with such a massive amount of debt – the £9 million from the council, £1 million from Colin simply as an overdraft, and about £5 million from HSBC. The turnover at the time was just under £4 million, so you can see we were massively geared. Fortunately we were able to bring in additional income streams – the pouring and the catering rights, the advertising around the stadium. And best of all we owned the ground.

'The starting-point was to look at a collaborative strategy, trying to build the club by entering into partnership with as many people as we could. The biggest one was Leeds Metropolitan University, using the Carnegie name. Leeds had set up a PE college, Carnegie College, early in the 20th century, using Andrew Carnegie money, but it was later absorbed into what became Leeds Polytechnic. That then became Leeds Metropolitan University, and the Carnegie name was suppressed because the new generation of universities wanted to be seen as competing with the red-brick universities. When Simon Lee came in as vice-chancellor in 2003, however, he saw Carnegie as being a big brand in sport and started using the university's privately generated funds on sponsorship and advertising. He entered into partnerships with Leeds rugby union team, the Irish and Scottish FAs and with Leeds United Ladies FC; Carnegie took over the sponsorship of the Rugby League Challenge Cup. With ourselves the premise was that Carnegie, by its association with Headingley and so with cricket, could appeal to overseas students from India, Pakistan, New Zealand and Australia whose tuition fees were two to four times that of UK students. As a result the return on the university's investment would be so much greater.

'It was a very successful collaborative strategy. We signed a naming-rights deal to be called Headingley Carnegie Stadium, and then a partnership agreement whereby we had a number of shared benefits. Player appearances, advertising around the ground, and in return we had access to sports psychologists, bio-mechanic and nutritional advice and all sorts of sports science equipment; use of the university gymnasium and its facilities when required. On the business side we have placement students doing PR, communications and marketing support, so it's quite an innovative partnership.

'We then went one step further by planning a dual-use pavilion with hospitality suites and a media centre. As part of our staging agreement we had to deliver players' facilities, media facilities, improved capacity, improved hospitality, and it was obvious from our balance sheet that we didn't have any money. We were borrowed up to the hilt. Our thinking was, how can we get someone else to fund the building and allow us to share it? So we talked to Leeds Met about how wonderful it would be for them to have a building in an international cricket ground, how a dual-use building could operate in the winter, when there was no cricket and students were in residence, and how it could operate in the summer, when there were no students for much of the time but cricket was being played. The overlap areas in April and September, we would manage that; we would live in harmony together. We also had some over-riding principles that said they cleared out when there was a Test match and gave us the building lock, stock and barrel.

'Once we reached agreement, the next thing was to put a funding plan in place. We got £4 million from Yorkshire Forward, the regional development agency, Leeds Met put up £14 million, and the club agreed to put in £3 million, which would be rentalised over 20 years. So we own the land but we've rented the rights to build on it to the university for 125 years. We pay them an annual maintenance fee to service and look after the building and we pay them what is effectively a rent, but that rent is simply writing off the £3 million capital investment. After 20 years we have 105 years of peppercorn rent and it's basically a free building. It's a fantastic deal for the club.'

Whether the pavilion is to everyone's taste depends on how Modernist you like your architecture. I enjoy it but then I'm not the Prince of Wales. Designed by SMC Alsop – Will Alsop was architect of the 2000 Stirling Prize winner, the Peckham Library in south London – the building's distinctive crystalline structure provides five floors of dual-use areas. So, for example, the tiered press box with its wide-vision view of the playing area and surrounding countryside, if not always in line with the pitch, is converted into a raked 150-seat lecture room out of season. Or maybe it's the other way round. Someone should certainly have whispered in the architect's ear that there's a naughty-step tendency among press corps that won't sit in one place for five minutes unless there's a deadline imminent. The press box configuration suggests that someone had in mind students who know their place for the duration of a lecture, which is considerably less than a day's play at a Test match. Still, that's just a journalist's grizzle, and we're all not as big as Derek Pringle.

There are two in-vision studios and two commentary rooms in which digital journalism students can experience first-hand a working media centre, while the hospitality suites convert into seminar rooms, and meeting rooms become match-day meeting spaces. A balcony of 570 premium seats allows Yorkshire to offer better-quality hospitality, which in turn means higher-value hospitality packages and higher-value tickets. The Americans have a saying for it: the nicer the nice the higher the price. And at £21 million there's no denying that the pavilion's price was certainly high. On the other hand the club paid only a small proportion of that, and the facilities satisfy the development plans within the staging agreement with the ECB. So maybe Stewart Regan was close to the mark when he described the Headingley Carnegie pavilion as a 'win-win' for Yorkshire.

Even so the story comes with a postscript – but not, one hopes, a parable. By the time the building opened in July 2010 Simon Lee, the Headingley Carnegie project's co-author, was no longer the university's vice-chancellor. He and the chancellor, former international distance runner and television commentator Brendan Foster, had stepped down a year and a half earlier during what the *Yorkshire Post* called a 'confusion of controversies'. These included the university's growing debt, 'a lack of public clarity surrounding the decision by governors to raise tuition fees', the fallout from the slump in property values and allegations by staff of a culture of bullying. Hardly was the building open than Stewart Regan announced he would be leaving Headingley at the end of the season to head up the Scottish Football Association. And about the time he was clearing his desk it was announced that the Archial Group, owners of SMC Alsop, had gone into administration after a falling out with HMRC over unpaid taxes. Given that things reputedly come in threes, be they Wise Men, wise monkeys, Stooges or Musketeers, Yorkshire County Cricket Club might have felt themselves in the clear. However, the size of their liabilities meant that their survival was by no means guaranteed – except by chairman Graves.

CHAPTER FOUR
HIGH ROAD, LOW ROAD

When we first met, Stewart Regan was just back from a Twenty20 fact-finding visit to India, along with Warwickshire's Colin Povey and Lancashire treasurer David Hodgkiss. His enthusiasm for what they saw at two Indian Premier League (IPL) games was apparent as he described the atmosphere in the stadiums. The noise levels from 55,000 screaming fans, the superb delivery of the events as a customer experience, the glamour encompassing a game of cricket, the strike-rates of 130 and 140 from the batting side. It was as if, like the visitor to the Soviet Union in 1919, he had seen the future and it worked. We now know what happened to that particular future. As for their own short-term future, all Regan and his fellow-travellers would see were flying feathers when his e-mail to the Test match grounds became public property, in the way e-mails invariably do. Its contents detailed their meeting in Delhi with IPL chairman and commissioner Lalit Modi and outlined a joint vision for an IPL-mirroring franchise circus in the United Kingdom.

If anything was guaranteed to spark the suspicions of the non-Test match counties that the Test match grounds were looking to break out of the 18-county construct, the F-word was a sure-fire favourite, the proverbial red rag to the small-town bulls. And the fall-out, when it came, was fast and furious, reverberating all the way back to India. ECB chairman Giles Clarke fired off his own e-mail to his opposite number on the Indian board, BCCI president Shashank Manohar, informing him of plans afoot to destroy the structure of world cricket and set up a rebel league. Regan's defenders were quick to point out that his e-mail threatened no such thing, which is true within a degree of interpretation. But it was also more than an account of some good old boys shooting the breeze in a Delhi curry house. The e-mail contained enough detail to put the wind up those who didn't get to have a dog in the race, especially as it showed that two IMG vice-presidents were also at the meeting. IMG, the global sports, entertainment and media group, defended their executives' attendance by saying that the group had set up the meeting with Modi at the English party's request. However, as IMG were a major player in helping the BCCI develop the IPL – conducting the sale of the franchises and handling the television production and distribution rights, the franchise rights, the sale of sponsorships, and the management of the events and venues – their presence suggested to the wary something more sinister than an exploratory gathering.

The venture that Regan outlined was based on the premise that the IPL would want to expand into the northern hemisphere because its southern hemisphere time frame was restricted by player availability, owing to international commitments determined by the ICC's Future Tours Programme. It was suggested that the ten existing IPL franchises might bid for ten new UK franchises based principally on the so-called Category A grounds – the major international grounds in England and Wales. The franchises would take 80 per cent of the commercial revenues, such as television rights, sponsorship and advertising, and the remaining 20 per cent would go to the counties staging the events. It was said that, 'IPL would GUARANTEE NOW a figure of $3 million to $5 million for each of us plus a staging fee for hosting the games if we were to support the idea. They are absolutely convinced we are sitting on a gold mine!'

The e-mail additionally provided more background on the dispute between the ECB and the IPL, which at the time was threatening the English clubs' participation in the 2010 Champions League – the multi-million dollar tournament that brought together the top-ranked Twenty20 teams from domestic competitions around the world. Sussex and Somerset were England's qualifiers when 12 teams contested the inaugural competition in 2009. The ECB, Australia and South Africa had been offered 16.67 per cent each of the equity in the competition, while India would hold the remaining 50 per cent on the grounds that 80 per cent of the revenue generated would come from India. It would appear that the ECB wanted a minimum of 25 per cent or there was no deal. There was no deal. Not only did the Board miss out on a share of the financial action but Hampshire and Somerset, that summer's Twenty20 finalists, missed out on playing in the Champions League because the Indian authorities moved it from October to dates in September which clashed with the County Championship.

History will relate if this latest impasse between the ECB and the IPL was a watershed as far as England's stake in world cricket is concerned. It was certainly a lost opportunity for the ECB to become shareholders in the Champions League venture, and the potential it might hold. Moreover, had they accepted the terms on offer, and had relations with the IPL been cemented as a result, much of the subsequent talk of English franchises and counties breaking away could have been averted. It was not one of the ECB's better moments.

One repercussion of Giles Clarke's e-mail to the BCCI was the suspension of Lalit Modi, the driving force behind the IPL. Truth be known, the knives were already out for him. Some Indian journalists were quietly predicting as much before Regan's e-mail put the IPL cat among the county-ground pigeons. In a country like India, creating something as huge, glamorous and successful as the IPL involves harnessing the patronage and resources of the most influential families and politicians. As often as not these can be one and the same. But in getting things done – and getting things done often means cutting corners – there's a correlative risk of alienating some other powerful group, or even alienating the people you think are your allies.

Modi had vision and a dynamic. He's typical of those men who push past whatever obstacles stand in their way. He took England's cricket-rooted notion of Twenty20, gave it a shot of American professional sports' pizzazz, added a twist of Bollywood glitz and gold, and shook it to an unprecedented level of high-rolling entertainment with player salaries to match. But his rise to power in India's cricket hierarchy attracted first envy and then enemies. Create a big beast like the IPL and in the end it can consume you. When Clarke's e-mail to the BCCI provided material cause for action, Modi's days were numbered, even if it took five months to count them down before he was deposed as chairman of the IPL Governing Council and as vice-president of the BCCI.

Former Kent captain Matthew Fleming, an ECB director and merchant banker, wasn't sure that Modi's going would affect the IPL, however. If anything, he thought, it might be just what it required. 'It needed a reality check to bring some corporate governance and process into it to enable international brands to invest in it with confidence and keep it going.'

Certainly the worldwide web had been awash with allegations of fraud, financial irregularities, money laundering, match fixing and illegal betting in connection with the IPL. In October 2010 the BCCI filed a complaint against Modi with the Mumbai police, alleging the misappropriation of funds, and there were also investigations into the alleged violation of foreign exchange regulations and tax offences relating to the IPL. It was claimed that Modi, by this time living in London, faced arrest if he returned to India. About the same time the BCCI staggered the cricket world by ending their agreement with two of the original IPL franchises, Rajasthan Royals, winners of the inaugural tournament in 2008, and Kings XI Punjab. In both instances the reason given was a violation of ownership and shareholder regulations; and in both instances, as we'll see in the next chapter, these franchises had been linked with English counties.

If Modi's fall from grace released an undeniable whiff of *Schadenfreude* back at the ECB, there was similarly a sweet smell of success around the non-TMGs at seeing off the second attempt in two years to smuggle franchises into English cricket. The first had come in the months that followed the launch of the IPL in 2008. The touchpaper that sparked the anger then was a discussion document, a franchise proposal, drawn up by MCC chief executive Keith Bradshaw and Surrey chairman David Stewart, along with the Lancashire and Hampshire chairmen. Their projection was that each franchise would be sold for £50 million, while the tournament itself might generate an annual income of £85 million from broadcasting rights, match-day sales and commercial revenue. Rod Bransgrove says with a laugh that his name was removed from the document 'because my name is inflammatory to some at ECB and we didn't want this important paper to be inflammatory'.

Some hope. Even without the Bransgrove imprimatur, any paper giving time to a nine-team English Premier League playing 57 games over 25 high-summer days couldn't fail to provoke an outcry. Especially as most of the games, maybe all of them, would be played at the Test match grounds. Not that Cardiff's potential inclusion as a Test match ground – it would stage its first Test in 2009 – cut any ice with the Glamorgan chairman, Paul Russell. He called the proposal, 'bootleg and divisive'. And with rumours rife that the proposal contained a proviso that the counties should have no direct involvement in the franchises, being called divisive was the least of its problems. The paper sounded downright radical.

Bransgrove argues otherwise. 'Despite all the assertions to the contrary, that Stewart-Bradshaw paper made it absolutely clear that the proposed competition was the property of all counties, not just the grounds it was staged at. And it made it even more clear that it was the property of all cricket, and not the ECB. In other words the money directly came into the game and was not subject to dilution by distribution through ECB.'

I may as well admit now that I have some sympathy for the franchise advocates. I was close to being one myself when I tried making a case for city cricket some years ago. You spend so much time ducking and weaving from the subsequent abuse that you wonder if facing

Holding and Roberts on a dark night would be preferable. But when you're considering how to bring investment into the game, as well as attract spectators to top-rank entertainment, a franchise operation offers a tried and tested template, even if the template was tried and tested in American sport. For a start a franchise allows you to build a brand, and Twenty20 cricket in England has still to achieve that, as several county chief execs admitted.

'We have to work very hard on delivering our Twenty20 because it's not yet right in this country,' Worcestershire's Mark Newton said. 'It's where most people want to watch a game, but there's a lot of work to do on it.'

'The truth is,' Bransgrove says, 'that with external, expert advice Bradshaw-Stewart concluded that you need two things to play cricket matches. You need a stage and you need players. We've got nine great stages in this country, and we've got at least 100 or so pretty good players. Then there are overseas players.'

Assuming the quality overseas players would be available now that international cricket has begun trampling all over English cricket's summer pastures. And assuming the non-Test match counties could be sure that franchise cricket was indeed a business model to sustain the 'have-nots' as well as the 'haves'. Their recent reactions suggest they can't be sure; some probably didn't want to be sure. Without so much as a press conference to place it in the public view, Bradshaw-Stewart bit the dust the moment it was leaked to the media, leaking to the media having gone from being a whistleblower's weapon to an everyday pastime. ('At some point it will be in the *Telegraph*,' Dave Brooks once told me with a grin. 'Most things are.') The visionaries, some would say the fantasists, got their heads back down below the parapet before the Shires backwoodsmen poured another pouch of grapeshot into their muskets.

'To have this aspiration that you're going to have an all-swinging, all-dancing product in the middle of summer which is going to attract everyone from the rest of the world, I'm afraid you're in cloud-cuckoo land,' said David East on a squally Southend afternoon when the only clouds in sight were bringing rain rather than cuckoos. 'So let's focus on making our Twenty20 a vibrant domestic tournament which is primarily for England-qualified players. Concentrate on what we know we can do well, or some of us can do well, which is deliver domestic Twenty20, an entertainment product in its own right, and maximise it.'

Essex definitely know how to maximise it. They promote their Twenty20 cricket aggressively. They have a target audience that includes Southend United and West Ham football fans. And if, as one visiting player declared, Chelmsford Friday nights are a bit of a bear-pit with 6,000 people packed in, it's nevertheless good-humoured and great fun. Friday night is party time. Asked if there was any secret to their success, David East said simply, 'We're marketing the hell out of it. We don't have any international distractions; we have a demographic that works. We have a niche in the market which we think appeals to the Chelmsford public. We start at seven o'clock, which means that people haven't got to lose work. In 35 minutes from Liverpool Street you can be in our ground and having a beer. The game's over by 9.45. We think we've got all the ingredients there for a successful product and we've demonstrated that it works.'

But at a sunny Old Trafford, Jim Cumbes was inclined to see things from a different perspective. He has a Test match ground to run, added to which his county, Lancashire, was one of those involved in the Bradshaw-Stewart paper. Not that he knew much about it at the time, as he explained. 'Our chairman dealt with it all because they kept it in a tight circle. But I know Keith [Bradshaw] was adamant that there were a lot of companies out there willing to back a franchise-based competition. Look, what we're saying is, the IPL is now the fourth-most successful sporting event in the world in terms of income, the crowds they get and so on. The problem is, the smaller clubs here in England don't have to fill 20,000 seats, they only have to fill five or six thousand. If our Test match grounds only had to fill five or six thousand they'd be perfectly happy with what's going on. Even so I think some of the smaller grounds are starting to struggle with crowds of even less than that because there's no spark in the competition.

'When they first started talking about four overseas players in a side, whether they were Indian or anyone else, at least that was different and would have had an attraction to the public. But there's no attraction now, and part of that is because a lot of counties, and I include ourselves in this, we've got overseas players coming in and players going out, they're here for three weeks, they're here for two games, there's no affinity with that. The supporters think, is he here next week or not? When you had overseas players for a season, there was some affinity. People watched Malcolm Marshall playing for Hampshire and they thought he was part of Hampshire. And now we've got an extra problem in that international cricket is played all the year round all over the world, when at one stage we were the only people playing cricket in our summer months.

'I still think there's a competition out there that's going to attract people who are not traditional cricket supporters. Some of the ideas that Keith Bradshaw and the others pulled together – the thrust of that was that the big grounds would stage the games with big-name players, some of whom might have been brought in from other counties, and there would be enough money made to (a) pay for what was required at the big grounds and (b) to give the smaller grounds, I don't know, a million quid a year. But the smaller grounds didn't want that because they weren't taking part.

'Now to a degree I can understand that. But by the same token, in difficult times, if you say to a Leicestershire or a Worcestershire, there's going to be a five-week window where there's going to be a competition, you're not going to be taking part in it although you could have your own competition if you want to, and at the end of it you get a cheque for a million pounds, I'd be inclined if I was a smaller club to say that's not a bad idea. That's what I need at the moment and I can still have my own Twenty20 competition, which is probably going to bring in four or five thousand people. But whether that will ever be acceptable is a moot point.'

It won't be if chief execs like East and Richard Gould have a say in the matter. Gould could hardly be more damning in his appraisal of the Test match grounds' apparent interest in setting up city-based leagues or Twenty20 franchises. It had nothing to do with the quality of county cricket, he said. It's all about money. 'It's everything to do with the servicing of debt levels that are unsustainable. The Test match grounds need more big games, they know there aren't enough Tests to go round, and if some of the smaller counties go by the wayside as a result, well, that's got nothing to do with them. I'm sorry but it has, it's got everything to do with them. It means we'd be changing the outlook of domestic cricket for the wrong reasons.'

So there we have it, the two sides of the coin. Not just the franchise coin but the county coin; the classic divide between the large grounds and the small, what in American football's National Football League (NFL) they call the big-market teams and the small-market teams. At least it's not quite the north-south divide along which England so often splits. But it does create conflict and it emphasises the absence of the 'all for one and one for all' philosophy that once underpinned county cricket.

'When I came into the game ten years ago,' Gloucestershire's Tom Richardson said, 'two chief executives told me we compete on the field but off it we all help each other. I don't think that rings quite as true now. There is less willingness to support each other. People tend to look after themselves a bit first.'

'I don't think that one-size-fits-all applies to cricket in the way people think it should. We've all got very different business models,' was how Richard Gould saw it.

Dogs eating dogs were mentioned more than once as I travelled around the country. The counties were even depicted as being their own worst enemies because in many ways they don't help themselves a great deal. They rarely work together when it comes to anything meaningful. Whether their franchise paper was meaningful or not, Keith Bradshaw and David Stewart have every reason to agree with that assessment, and good reason to reflect on whether the counties as a sporting group have a clue as to the direction they should be taking their game.

'Our franchise proposal was devised with the future in mind,' Bradshaw told Cricinfo's Andrew Miller in 2010, 'and unfortunately the future is hurtling towards us on an early train.' Stewart, meanwhile, countered claims that their proposal would have cut out the smaller grounds in favour of the major grounds, telling Miller, 'We always saw it as a partnership of the 18 counties. We didn't see it as the nine big grounds going it alone and leaving the others deserted. But it was, let's say, ahead of its time.'

Well, as Harold Wilson once said of politics, what isn't presentation is timing. And while the Bradshaw-Stewart proposal may have got its timing wrong, its presentation – albeit pre-empted by the press – was also on the shaky side in Mark Newton's opinion. Having spent eight years at The Oval earlier in his career, he was better placed than some chief executives to empathise with the demands a Test match county has to contend with. His take on a franchise-based EPL was less dismissive than that of some colleagues. But he nonetheless thought the way the proposal was handled 'was a shambles. It could have been very simple. If they had said to all 18 counties, we promise you an extra half-million pounds, they'd have had instant agreement. Half a million quid for each of you but we want only nine franchises. You Worcestershire, you work with Warwickshire, you play half the games there and half the games here [at New Road] to start with. There's nothing the ECB could have done about that, and they'd probably have been delighted to have it taken off their hands. I would if I'd been chief executive of the ECB.'

The unknown factor in all this is the degree of public support there'd be for a franchise-based tournament in England. Did the product really have a ready market to fill the large-capacity Test match grounds, or was the speculation being driven by all the noughts that media rights and the sale of franchises had realised for the IPL and its owner, the BCCI? Eight franchises sold for around $720 million when the IPL was launched in 2008, and there was a further $703.3 million when two new franchises were auctioned off two years later. Global broadcasting rights over ten years were valued at anything from $1.6 billion to $2.4 billion, depending on which sources you referred to and who was doing the interviews. In the context of county cricket they're astronomical figures, and all things being unequal it's unlikely an English Premier League could have matched them. It would end up being *Wall Street* without Michael Douglas. Still, you never know, and no one did know for sure because it never got that far.

David Smith for one is sure that franchises had no future, and not only because at least half the counties opposed them. 'I think as a country we're very tribal and, having watched the failure of region-alisation in rugby, what we actually associate with is clubs – Kent v Leicestershire or Derbyshire v Nottingham. South-East Eagles versus, let's say, London Dolphins, that for me won't work, and I think the novelty would die very quickly. East Midlands v West Midlands would have some novelty value if you've got, let's say, five overseas players in each team, but I don't think it would work long term. You'd have to market the game in a totally different way to get people to buy into that. I'm not certain that we as a country…

'I can see it in India, cricket's their number one game, though I wouldn't hold the IPL up as being a fantastic standard of cricket. It's been an interesting spectacle, driven by the overseas players in a cricket-mad country. But I'm not certain commercially that it can work without the television money. I think it's become a bit of a toy for the rich to have a franchise in India, and there are some very rich people there. But I'm not seeing anything that says to me we've got to map that model out because it will generate X or Y million pounds. We have to be very careful, and do our due diligence properly, before we buy into a franchise format that might not work anywhere other than in India.

'For a start I don't have any doubt that investors in this country would want a return on their money, whereas I'm not sure the Indian franchises see it quite the same. It's a completely different culture: the cricket there is linked to the movie industry and everything else to do with the entertainment industry. It's status and everything else that goes with that. I'm not certain that appeal would be quite the same in this country. People here would be driven by the bottom line and what they could get out of it. I don't think any bank or anybody else would invest without seeing an exit strategy, and what that exit strategy was going to deliver.

'Clearly the nine Test match grounds, because of their size, see themselves being the main players. But I think there's a misconception. Some of them think the England players and other international players will be available. I'm not convinced. I can't see that, within the only break of the year, international cricketers are going to play in the UK for four weeks unless it is significantly worthwhile. People were horrified in the setting-up of our T20 when... I had a conversation with Dhoni as to how much he was going to cost, and he wasn't going to come for less than a million pounds. Now as soon as you do that for Dhoni, all the England players will want to renegotiate with their counties. You're not going to get Stuart Broad turn up for, I don't know, a quarter of a million pounds when Dhoni's on a million. You'll have absolute mayhem in terms of getting a salary budget together that's going to work, even with a salary cap like they've got in India. That's why you're getting the local Indian players coming in, the lesser quality Indian players, because they're trying to balance the top players' salaries. So that's another thing we need to be aware of.'

Smith's estimation of the country being tribal chimes in with the remarks of political commentators in the immediate aftermath of the 2010 general election, when no party achieved an outright mandate to govern. When not greeted with scorn, talk of a coalition government was met with doubt as to whether the British (read English) were ready for it, being by nature as tribal in their politics as they were in their football or their cricket, their rugby or… just about everything. 'Them and us; Us and them' was part of the national psyche. I am as much defined by what you are and I am not; of what I am and you are not. The game's not necessarily the thing.

Some century and a half ago Matthew Arnold proposed that in England it was important to belong or affiliate to certain institutions in order to be part of the national life. Arnold, being a man of his time, had in mind bodies such as the Church of England or Oxford and Cambridge Universities. Today he might have included MCC, and even county clubs and football teams. But back when he was writing *Culture and Anarchy* there were only eight counties playing what is now considered first-class cricket. And Aston Villa, Manchester United and the like were still on the far side of the steppes. Today they're the focus of the affiliations that many would see as reflecting the national life of England, probably ahead of religious and political beliefs.

Players move from clubs and counties but fans and supporters don't. Their affections are less likely to change than the club or county they support might change, because these affiliations are not simply individual ties. They are the consequence of long-established enmities, age-old rivalries, inherited or assumed in homes, neighbourhoods and school playgrounds. They're part of the collective memory of growing up, providing the continuance of a sense of identity.

It's not something I've inherited or adopted. There's no football team, no county, whose result or scorecard I first look for when I open a newspaper, turn on the television or go online. It's probably why I never responded to the magic of *Fever Pitch*, so perfectly pitched for a generation of youngish middle-class males struggling to find a sense of identity in a changing England. What better swap than a college scarf for a football one.

But that's just a rim-dweller's viewpoint; of someone who has never felt the need to place his home in any certain location, be it town or country. For me home is more a concept than a sentiment. The Spanish-American philosopher, George Santayana, didn't believe it was good for one's moral integrity to live anywhere but home for any length of time, unless one lived there with a sense of exile. So I don't know what that says about my moral integrity. I've lived in England for many years without feeling like an exile or without feeling it's my home. And while I enjoy living here, I nevertheless retain my immigrant's eye for reading between the lines, searching out the nuances, the symbols and the divisions which the locals lock into from birth and which often lock out the incomer, the outsider. It's why on the one hand I can appreciate that there's a case for thinking franchises might yet become a successful business model for English cricket, even if not on the scale of the IPL, and on the other hand understand that they can't. It's the dilemma of compromise, the devil in coalition, the belief, occasionally disillusioned, that the English are able to live in the present looking to the future as well as to the past.

Take innovation. It's one of Britain's great achievements. So is the entrepreneurial spirit, although for some reason the two don't get along as much as they used to. Different hymnals, maybe. Possibly the entrepreneurs have grown flabby from making money out of money instead of helping bring to fruition the inventiveness that drives economies. Designers, it used to be said, had to go to Scandinavia to get their ideas manufactured and marketed; scientists, it is still said, head off to the United States to fund their future. Maybe they're urban myths, but then again, said Tom Wilkie in *British Science and Politics since 1945*, 'the British are good at inventing things, but poor at turning them into products that customers would like to buy.' This was, he said, a prevailing British disease.

Which is why it took a foreign businessman to recognise the potential of the Twenty20 prototype, to bring in film and television personalities as investors, to add on apps such as fashion shows and ticketed after-match parties, to encourage women to the games in big numbers. In fact to turn the cricket not into just another game but into an event. 'Cricketainment' the Indians call it. They've hijacked the language as well. Not that the Indians get to run away with all the plaudits when it comes to Twenty20. Trent Bridge put on a good show when they staged the ICC World Twenty20 in 2009.

'It was a great success,' Derek Brewer said. 'It wasn't just that we attracted many of our existing supporters who enjoy all forms of the game; we attracted a new audience as well. It was an incredibly demanding tournament for the team here to run, but because the cricket was superb and the event was different, people came to watch.

'I'm a traditionalist at heart and was brought up on County Championship cricket. But we must ensure that we're always looking ahead, challenging the conventional wisdom and thinking differently. So in redeveloping Trent Bridge, for instance, we have tried to match maintaining our outstanding heritage with modernity. The same principle should apply to the structure of the game as well.'

Those of us who had played 20-over cricket in evening leagues for clubs and pubs in earlier decades never gave Twenty20 much cred as an innovation when the First-Class Forum voted for it in April 2002; there was nothing so very new in it. Mini-cricket formats had been tried elsewhere, New Zealand for example, and hadn't come to much. However, the new format was a step into the unknown for county cricket, something of a gamble even, and for a conservative group like the counties that was innovation enough. The inventive spirit that could have made Twenty20 a money-spinning brand in its own right would have been a step too far, especially so soon in the new millennium. Not that a proposal for franchises would have come completely out of left field. Someone had suggested as much, for a one-day tournament, at the time of the 1999 World Cup in England. It just didn't get Lord's a-leaping any more then than it did ten years later.

The ECB's Twenty20 game plan was to give the struggling counties a boost by attracting a new audience to cricket. And it worked. They'd done their homework: they'd spent £200,000 of their limited resources on research and another £250,000 on marketing. They'd come up with a product that brought people into the grounds again. There was pop music, there was occasionally some rock, there were bouncy castles, jacuzzis, fairground rides and, well, all the fun of the fair. County cricket had seen nothing quite like it before, even if, to be honest, it felt more Blackpool than Bollywood. And you knew the English game was going down the wrong road when the ECB's man at the heart of the new format, Stuart Robertson, declared that, 'Twenty20 is not an end in itself, but a means to an end. The hope is that a 20-over game after work or school will be the first rung on a cricket-watching ladder that has a Championship game at its top.'

You could Google galore and still not find a reference to Lalit Modi hoping that the IPL would have Indians queuing around the North-East Frontier Railway Stadium to watch Assam battle it out with Orissa for first-innings points in the Ranji Trophy, Elite Group B. For Modi, the entrepreneur, the visionary, the opportunist, the ladder was reaching for the sky. He was building a brand; the ECB was selling baby food.

'Surely, as we started Twenty20,' Jim Cumbes almost pleaded, 'we must be able to do better than we're doing at the moment. I'm not saying we'll do as well as the IPL, but I still think there's a good idea out there which is a T20 competition that's going to attract large crowds.'

It's this hope of attracting large crowds that has me wondering if IPL-style franchise cricket would work in England now, particularly if there's a question mark over the availability and the cost of the top overseas cricketers. Who's going to attract these large crowds? Even more to the point, who's going to attract the investors? There was no name sponsor when Twenty20 began in 2003 – there were sponsorship partners, as I understand it – although, as Jim Cumbes explained, it was hoped that a major consumer brand would eventually come on board. 'All the chief execs agreed that the sponsor for Twenty20's got to be modern because that's what we're aiming at. We're not aiming at cricket lovers here; we're aiming at FMCGs, the fast-moving consumer goods people. So, is there a Tesco out there, is there a Sainsbury?'

A good question. Because who happens along when the ECB announce their name sponsor? Friends Provident, a financial services outfit previously associated with the done, dusted and dust-binned 50-over competition. Totally the wrong image for the Twenty20 game, and sporting a lower-case 't20' logo to boot. There was a successful businesswoman who, when she set up her first company, used lower-case lettering on her stationery 'because I didn't have any capital'. Were the ECB and Friends Provident letting us in on something with their little 't', or was it just that they were off the pulse when it came to choosing a logo? I'm sure someone was paid a lot of money for it.

'It was right that banking and finance were associated with Championship cricket,' Cumbes said, 'but not this competition which was glorified baseball, if you like. [Steady on, Jim, some of us enjoy baseball.] You want somebody out there, a big modern firm, that can brand the game and get some return for it.'

It's wishful thinking. If big-name brands were going to get involved in county Twenty20 they'd be there already. Top-market brands want to be linked with top-of-the-range products, which in English cricket terms is the international game. A franchise tournament might have whetted a new commercial appetite for a different kind of cricket product, but because of self-interest, protectionism, conservatism, call it what you will, the stumps were drawn before the first ball was bowled. Not that the idea will go away. Third time could be third time lucky, not necessarily because all 18 counties have had a change of heart but because the alternative will be too scary for the game to contemplate. Franchises might be the necessary evil – and for some counties the last throw of the dice in the Last Chance saloon.

CHAPTER FIVE
GRAND DESIGNS

No surprise then that the Test match counties' flirtation with franchises fell foul of their non-Test match brethren. 'All for one and one for all', as the Three Musketeers vowed, is just the stuff of fiction after all. And not very English when you think of it. Much too French, like the Common Market, eating snails and batting with both legs front on to the bowler. All very foreign. The English would sooner send out some m'lord chappy to rout the enemy. The Scarlet Pimpernel, Ted Dexter or David Gower. Though there was something of Athos and Porthos about Ian Botham and 'Freddy' Flintoff: men of steel as well as hearts of oak.

But back to the counties and collaboration. Any hint of the Test match grounds getting together to form a consortium or establish a power bloc has always drawn a negative response from the smaller counties. It's a reaction that has suited the game's mandarins, whether of old the MCC, later the TCCB, and now the ECB. If your bureaucracy is built upon the central administration maintaining control over policy and events, the last thing you want is a powerful cadre of independent counties. Which is what would have happened with a franchise model underwriting the business plans of the Test match grounds.

Ideally the management of the franchise tournament would have been outside the day-to-day operation of the ECB, even if ownership of the product resided in the ECB in the way that ownership of the IPL rests with the BCCI. It would need to have its own board and so on, I was told, otherwise it would get lost in the other competitions. Better for the bureaucrats, then, if there are dependent, even weak, satellites relying on them to negotiate for the income streams from television rights and sponsorships that keep the smaller counties afloat. Or so the theory goes. The counties don't recognise themselves as weak or dependent or satellites. They see themselves as 18 separate entities.

Even among the major grounds, not everyone was convinced that the time had come for franchises. Questions remained unanswered as to who would buy them, and what rights the counties might have to surrender. If potential owners wanted English cricket to go down the franchise route, some were asking, how come they were keeping a low profile? Also uncertain was the essential matter of television rights, currently contracted by the ECB to BSkyB for all international and domestic cricket. Stewart Regan in his incendiary e-mail to fellow Test match grounds was reduced to asking if any of his recipients had a copy of the ECB-Sky agreement. All round it had had the makings of a very cockeyed revolution. Tanks on the Nursery Ground it was not.

Colin Povey, who accompanied Regan to the Modi meeting, thought the franchise concept was interesting 'in principle', but he was not convinced it was the best solution to English cricket's financial quandary. Apart from anything else, Britain's sporting heritage and tradition left many sports lovers with an aversion to franchises as a club business model, in the same way that many strongly opposed the commercialisation of sport. Another aspect of franchise sport Povey suspected the English public wouldn't buy was the scrapping of promotion and relegation, even though this was comparatively new in cricket and still had its critics. For franchise owners, security of tenure creates value, whereas the threat of relegation brings investor uncertainty. Club supporters may not enjoy the prospect of relegation but there's a pleasure of sorts, nonetheless, in watching your team struggle for survival, just as the following season there might be a different kind of pleasure in watching them fight for promotion.

'To pretend you're going to create hugely valuable cricket franchises in the UK in the medium term, let alone in the short term, is pie in the sky,' Povey said. 'There may be some who see a golden opportunity for English cricket in the IPL model, but I'd take a lot of convincing that a Birmingham franchise has more value and appeal over a successful Warwickshire and Edgbaston in a well structured and scheduled calendar.'

Added to which, he implied, a Twenty20 initiative that was no more than a short-term staging agreement for IPL games in England was never going to be the elixir the Test match grounds were looking for. All that the grounds could be sure of were the costs.

'Most of the money will go back to India and we'll just be a venue. Next time they might go to South Africa or somewhere else.'

Even so, in spite of his doubts, Povey did not rule out some kind of affiliation with the IPL and BCCI. At one time there had been talk of Warwickshire linking up with Kings XI Punjab, one of the two IPL franchises since expelled by the BCCI. Hampshire talked of going into partnership with the other, Rajasthan Royals, Shane Warne being the common denominator in that particular ménage. The Warwickshire initiative didn't get far, however, foundering in the wake of the Regan e-mail and Lalit Modi's demise.

'If you look at global cricket and who's driving all the money,' Povey said, 'it's India. Who's driving the next biggest slice of the cake? England. So if the ECB and the BCCI could work together effectively we could possibly bring more money into our domestic game for the good of everyone – all 18 counties, the women's game, the recreational game. It would be an opportunity to reinvigorate and enhance our traditional values and put them into a more contemporary setting.'

The setting he was thinking of was one that reflected Birmingham's multi-cultural make-up, and in particular its large Asian population. Something like 50 per cent of the children playing cricket within the Warwickshire Cricket Board framework are from an Asian background, whereas the county club's membership is more traditional, being older, whiter and, for the time being, more affluent. 'If we can take the profile of our youth cricket,' Povey says with fervour, 'and bring it forward so that those kids don't fall away from the game, as you might suggest they're doing at the moment; if we can keep them associated with the county club, and with Edgbaston as a venue; if some partnership between the BCCI and the IPL, the ECB and Warwickshire County Cricket Club helps to facilitate this, then to me that sets us up for a much healthier trading environment going forward.'

In the meantime, 'We have to face up to how we deal with the fundamentals of our sport. We've got a great heritage but we're under-exploiting, under-leveraging, under-utilising it. Until we fix some of the fundamentals of what we offer people, both in the fabric of the ground for their match-day experience and the quality of the cricket that's played, we're fiddling while Rome burns. Unless we wake up to looking at our game not from the players' and administrators' viewpoint but from the punters', the consumers' point of view, we have a serious problem. But if we have a consistently successful England team and a genuinely vibrant, competitive and sensibly scheduled domestic game for the first-class counties, there'll be a lot less heat in the talk about creating franchises.'

At Edgbaston, improving the match-day experience for cricketers and customers centres on the ground's £30 million makeover, all part of Warwickshire's ambitious master plan to position the ground and the city of Birmingham at the forefront of international cricket. At the heart of the development are a new pavilion, club offices and banqueting and conference suites in a state-of-the-art wrap either side of a revamped entrance concourse. All told it means a ground-capacity increase from around 21,000 to 25,000. Birmingham City Council pledged £20 million of this capital investment project through a long-term fixed-interest loan. The balance came from the commercial development of land that Warwickshire already owned on the perimeter of the ground; what is known as an 'enabling development'. Advantage West Midlands, the local regional development agency, put up the money for that and Warwickshire will eventually repay them with the proceeds from the commercial development. The overall borrowing was expected to take 30 years to pay back.

Why all this borrowing and capital investment at a time of uncertainty in both cricket's and the nation's economy? And what are local authorities doing, lending money to cricket clubs at a time of cuts in government spending and public sector jobs? Is this really what public funds are for? A lot of it is down to the ubiquitous TSF2, the ECB's Facility Policy and Requirement Strategy document that sets out the standards that grounds must meet to be rated either Category A (Tests, one-day internationals and county games), Category B (one-day internationals and county games) or Category C (county, England Lions and Under-19 games, tour matches and women's internationals). TSF2 gave the counties until 2011 to comply, and developments like those at Edgbaston and elsewhere don't get off the ground overnight. There are meetings with architects, discussions over drawings and revisions, consultations with local authority planners, neighbouring residents' fears and objections to placate and overcome, more revisions to drawings, loans, grants and other financing to arrange, county members to consult, the local authority planning meeting ... and even once the plans are approved by the local councillors there's always the possibility of the development being 'called in' by the Department for Communities and Local Government. The economic downturn that followed the 2008 credit crunch was not even a tinkle on the Treasury's porcelain when some of these developments were being discussed. And it's not as if standing still was an option.

'Certainly we were scared of the immediate downside of not having international cricket if we didn't do the development,' Povey explained. 'The reason for the scale is two-fold. One is to make a stunning success of the international cricket we stage; the second is to give us facilities we can sell on a regular commercial basis on the 300-odd days of the year when the stadium's idle as a cricket venue.'

As for the local authorities bankrolling stadium development, someone has to do it. Povey is adamant that Warwickshire would not have raised the kind of money they needed on the commercial market, and the ECB's contribution to capital investment in grounds – £24 million for the period 2008 to 2012 – is a mere ripple in the 18-counties pond. It certainly palls when compared with the $700 million that the NFL loaned American football clubs over ten years to help build or improve their stadiums. And as American sports journalist Mark Yost points out in his intriguingly titled *Tailgating, Sacks, and Salary Caps*, 'the majority of the stadium-building boom has been financed by the taxpayers, most of whom will never see the inside of an NFL stadium.' Yost figures the average taxpayer contribution to be 'relatively constant at about 65 per cent'. The average taxpayer doesn't always get his money back either.

Here, as in America, city corporations commission economic impact studies to support the argument that sport adds value to a region's commercial and social life. We'll look later in the chapter at the local authority thinking that helped fund improvements at Trent Bridge.

Taking Warwickshire as a business, as opposed to simply a cricket club, there's a long-term logic to their master plan. Just how sound that logic is, time alone will tell. For the moment, given cricket's current state of uncertainty, with the game heavily reliant on television income, it makes sense to build a more balanced portfolio of revenues so that the club and the ground are not entirely dependent on international cricket. Or on the weather, come to that. Warwickshire have been fortunate, as Povey and his chairman admit, to have in Birmingham City Council and Advantage West Midlands two benevolent backers who share their vision. Where doubts rise are in their medium- to long-term ability to service the debt they're committed to. One of Povey's fellow chief execs calculates Warwickshire's annual interest bill to be around £1.3 million. If correct, that's more than their record pre-tax profit for 2009.

Furthermore the business plan is based on Edgbaston getting a decent crack at staging international cricket, and it assumes that Warwickshire's commercial department gets full value out of selling the new banqueting and conference facilities on non-match days. Both assumptions are a big ask, and could prove to be too big. There's no guarantee these days that any ground has a right to Test cricket, as Povey pointed out. 'Old Trafford, remember, had an Ashes Test provisionally allocated to them in 2009. Then Cardiff came in as a new Test match venue, bid a fortune for an Ashes game and got it. Old Trafford missed out. This immediately put places like ourselves, Trent Bridge, Old Trafford and Headingley in a most uncomfortable position because now we had new entrants coming into the market who were going to displace us as Test match venues if we didn't upgrade our grounds. With major investment in our stadium we think we have a compelling case for staging international cricket in Birmingham, whichever way the ECB's Major Match Group divvies up the allocation of matches.'

Just how essential international cricket is to the major grounds becomes apparent when comparing what happened to Edgbaston and Old Trafford in 2009. Warwickshire with an Ashes Test cashed in, and Edgbaston also had a one-day international against West Indies and the Twenty20 Finals day. Cricket's net contribution to their record profit of £1,156,396, up £709,693 on 2008, was more than a million pounds. The previous year they had recorded a net loss on cricket, in spite of staging a one-day international against New Zealand and a Test against South Africa. The Test match attendance figures throw some light on that: 59,436 for South Africa, 101,538 for the Australians. There's nothing to beat a household brand name like the Ashes when it comes to marketing. Or maybe the English happen to enjoy the prospect of Australians being beaten.

For Lancashire, missing out on an Ashes Test, and even a one-day international, was a significant factor in their pre-tax loss of £605,099, against a pre-tax profit of £258,664 the year before when they had one of the seven Tests. Income was down across the board in 2009: match receipts, executive box rentals, advertising (by 73 per cent), catering and even the hotel, the Old Trafford Lodge. Having two sell-out Twenty20 internationals against Australia was no compensation: both were washed out, though presumably the rain insurance would have covered that. The thing about the wham-bam games is that they're over too quickly to earn significant money on bar sales and catering, or even ground advertising. The boards don't get as much television exposure as in the longer formats. Makes sense really; just doesn't make so much money.

What brought home some bacon for Lancashire were five days of sell-out Take That concerts and a Coldplay gig that between them grossed almost £2 million: that was 15.8 per cent of Lancashire's overall income and worth close on a million pounds after costs. What with the hotel, conferencing, car parking for the other Old Trafford when Manchester United play at home and their concerts, you might wonder why Lancashire bother with cricket at all. Their new conference centre, The Point, already had around a million pounds in bookings for six to nine months when it opened in 2010 – and it also gave the ground 2,500 additional seats for watching cricket.

In fact, why invest something in the region of £32 million, as Lancashire are, to build a new pavilion and two new stands, as well as re-orientate the playing square so that play isn't disrupted when the late-afternoon sun shines down on Manchester? There's probably a nice little business opportunity in reducing the size of the ground, playing only county cricket and, with their diversity of non-cricketing income streams, becoming a successful county club that wins some Championship titles. The members would enjoy that; they've been waiting long enough.

'Hang on a minute,' Jim Cumbes said, 'this is Manchester, Old Trafford, 150 years of history, it's the north-west. If we're going to promote cricket it's in places like this that we have to get people interested. But we need the certainty of international matches and right now we've lost that certainty.

'When the games were allocated, before the bidding system came in, there wasn't a problem. We always knew Lord's and The Oval would get a Test match, that was written down, and everybody understood and accepted it. That left the four other grounds, Old Trafford, Trent Bridge, Headingley and Edgbaston, and you knew once every four years you were going to miss a Test match. So you planned for it, and then you were back on track the next three years. Furthermore, in your off year, the Board gave you a supplement because you'd missed out. I think the last club to get that was Trent Bridge and they received, I think it was £400,000, as compensation for not having a Test match. So they were able to continue with what they wanted to do with their ground, even though they hadn't got a Test.'

The bid process, with grounds entering a blind bid to stage international matches or major domestic events such as the Twenty20 Finals day, came in with the emergence of grounds such as Durham's Riverside, Hampshire's Rose Bowl and Glamorgan's Swalec Stadium as venues with Test match aspirations. Some among the traditional Test match grounds have viewed the bid process as a dash for cash by a greedy governing body, and there's certainly evidence of the cash cow putting in the hours at the milking parlour. In 2006 the ECB received £5.4 million from the grounds in major match bidding fees. This rose to £9.7 million in 2007, £14.3 million in 2009, dropped to £12.2 million in 2010 and rocketed to an anticipated £17.5 million in 2011. It's just like Robin Hood, muttered one aggrieved Test match county executive (not Nottinghamshire's), taking from the wealthy grounds to pay for the poor.

Given the debt levels, the word 'wealthy' owes more to the Robin Hood analogy than the reality of the balance sheet. But there's no denying that the grounds, even the new venues, believe they have been squeezed so hard by the ECB that there has been nothing spare to service the facilities improvements that the ECB expect. It is hardly surprising then that some county administrations started casting envious eyes over the IPL wall.

'Clubs are certainly concerned that their money-generating cricket is costing them more and more because of the bid fee,' Colin

Povey said, 'while at the same time those days of cricket have become less and less certain because of the way the process operates. So the grounds start thinking that they've got this huge commercial pressure to service and repay borrowings. They have to find new revenues from somewhere and here's a model that's different. Being a franchise venue might enable me to hang on to more money than I'm getting from the traditional model, which by the way is costing three times as much as it did in the past and with no certainty that I'll get anything in a year's time. Well,' Povey added, 'something has to give.'

However, there has been more to the bid process than money alone. The bidding counties have to meet the criteria of the ECB balanced scorecard, which allocates points to different categories. Another box-ticking exercise? Not really. The scorecard allows the wise men on the ECB's Major Match Group to find a number closest to the number they've already thought of. Theirs is 100, and each county's bid would be assessed against that.

Counties bidding for a one-day international in 2011, say, would have been scored like this. The bid money itself had a weighting of 20, so bids would have received X points out of 20 according to the rest of the bids. Other points categories on the scorecard include ECB infrastructure requirements, hotel and hospitality costs, transport links and parking, stand accommodation and public facilities, floodlights, media facilities, international match-days the previous year, and major match-days at other grounds within 50 miles. Finally there's the cost of tickets, with, perversely, more points allocated for lower priced tickets for under-16s.

With the money going into the ECB's coffers being such a potent element in the process, clubs knew there was no point putting in a low bid because it would rank low on the scorecard. 'You bid high because you'd rather earn £50,000 as earn nothing, whereas what you need to earn is £500,000,' said Durham's David Harker.

But as Jim Cumbes pointed out, 'You also get points for low-priced tickets. So I've said, "Hang on a minute, you want so much in bid money for the game and at the same time you're saying we can't bring that much in through the gate to pay for it." So where do we get it from? It's crackers.'

Nonetheless Cumbes would be the first to agree that ticket prices should be lower. 'We get a stack of money off television, £75 million a year or whatever it is now; we should be charging people £40 to come to a Test match, not a hundred quid. I don't think it's right, but at the same time we have to pay our bills.'

Someone ultimately has to pay for the bid fee: the poor old punter whose ticket is loaded with a share of the bid along with all the other elements included in the price. It's the cost of competition in the international-match marketplace, and that competition is anything but straightforward. For a start it's compromised by the staging agreements for games that the Board can award grounds for anything up to five years in advance, although the norm is usually three years. Nor is the process helped by the privileged position that Lord's has in the distribution of matches. The ground is virtually guaranteed a Test match against each touring team because the visitors expect to play there. Let's face it: there'd be a diplomatic kerfuffle of gunboat proportions were a touring side denied a 'Lord's Test'. And that's just the reaction of the MCC members; heaven knows what they'd make of it in Johannesburg and Jodhpur. Not that it's a likely scenario. As one MCC insider put it, 'If we were really shitty about it we could put in an offer that means we get all the Test matches.'

If that sounds unlikely, it's only because over the river The Oval has a long-term staging arrangement that seems to stretch past Peckham and beyond the outskirts of Penge. Boycott batting on a belter wouldn't have been as eternal. Come rain or shine Surrey get their Test match; London gets at least two a year and as often as not it has three. The staging agreements impacted on the bidding process in another way as well. Clubs already guaranteed a Test match for a certain year could cross-subsidise bids, using the money they expected to earn from their staging-agreed game to bid for other major matches that same year.

'During my six years as a chief executive,' a pragmatic Derek Brewer told me, 'the level of competition for staging major matches has increased significantly, and that very tough competitive environment has reaped benefits in the form of better facilities and enhanced returns to the ECB. However, I was brought up with competition in my previous role and we have to focus on what we can control. That means ensuring that our expenditure matches our income. It's important that we undertake robust scenario planning so we can meet our future challenges and capitalise on the opportunities that come our way. There is certainly no reason why Nottinghamshire in particular and cricket in general should be immune from competitive forces.'

The question no one seemed to ask when the bid process was introduced, seemingly no one at the ECB, was whether the Test match grounds could continue to sustain the flow of funds to the centre. Time soon came up with an answer, however, and in not too long a time at that. They couldn't. While competitive bidding for major matches shored up the ECB's finances in the short term, it did so to the medium- and long-term disadvantage of the counties. Financially, I was told more than once, and not only by Test match counties, 'the game is in a real mess'. Few thought that the ECB had considered the bid process strategically. It was all about – that expression again – the dash for cash and early in 2011 the ECB bowed to the inevitable, announcing that they would review the process by which major matches were allocated.

The major match grounds are not the sole cause for concern, however. The smaller grounds have benefited from the ECB's Robin Hood tendency of raising revenue through the bid process and distributing the booty around all the counties. But what happens if the Test match grounds can no longer afford to pay? Or refuse to pay, as Yorkshire intimated in 2011 when they said they would not be bidding for an Ashes Test in 2013 or 2015? The stakes were simply too high, chairman Colin Graves explained, and he was not prepared to put the club at risk by bidding between one and two million pounds to have an Australian Test at Headingley. Yorkshire, announcing huge losses for 2010, reckoned it had cost them in the region of a million pounds to stage that year's neutral Test between Australia and Pakistan, which not only was all over inside four days but failed to attract more than quarter-capacity crowds on any of them. No wonder Mark Tagg at Northamptonshire found the whole bidding situation 'scary. My concern as a small county is if the overall staging fees are reduced, that will certainly impact on us.'

Ask around the counties when the crunch might come and several point immediately to 2013, the year when, were the ECB to continue with the bid process, there would be four grounds bidding for two Ashes Tests. In fact it would have been five, had Yorkshire not folded their cards and walked away from the table. On top of this, or bubbling nicely underneath, the current Sky rights deal ends in 2013, and the government's public sector spending cuts will have drawn serious blood. Each year the ECB produce a Financial Report on the previous year, based on figures provided by the first-class counties, but if there's anything that matches the forward-looking 'robust scenario planning' which Derek Brewer mentioned earlier, we don't hear much about it.

Apparently, however, the ECB have not committed themselves to recreational funding levels beyond 2013, which is when their current Sport England agreement ends – along with the Sky contract. That sounds like unfortunate timing. Of the £20 million or so that went into the recreational game in 2010, more than a quarter came from Sport England, so who's to say the ECB won't transfer some of their responsibilities from the centre to the counties if the funds run short? That'll be a further pressure on the counties' finances, and what will suffer is all the community and grass-roots work they've been doing.

Work in the community, and not necessarily cricket-related activities, plays an important part in Nottinghamshire's business plan. It helped them fund their ground development at Trent Bridge for a start, as Derek Brewer explained. 'Back in 2006 we were faced with a real dilemma. Despite all the excellent work instigated by my prede-cessors, Mark Arthur and David Collier, in redeveloping Radcliffe Road and Fox Road respectively, there was a real imperative to rede-velop the old West Wing and Parr stands. We were spending more than £50,000 a year just on maintenance, and additionally the ECB had set out in TSF2 the "model ground" criteria we had to adhere to in order to stage major matches in the future. These included the need for permanent floodlights, a permanent replay screen, a world-class control facility and a pitch-viewing facility for ICC officials.

'While our financial position was very sound, thanks to years of excellent stewardship from executive and committee members alike, we certainly did not have sufficient resources to finance an £8.2 million ground development. So, given the strength of our local partnerships, we went out and obtained funding of £6.2 million from external sources, putting in the other £2 million ourselves. We obtained a grant of £2.5 million from the East Midlands Develop-ment Agency [emda] and loans of £1.23 million each from our three local authorities.

'What at that stage was different about the loan arrangements was the scale of our community commitment in return for a competitive deal. The benefits programme includes such things as promotional appearances by players and officials to support local initiatives, cricket development roadshows in the city, county and borough, tickets to schools for county matches and visits from our cricket development officers to local schools.'

Keeping international cricket at Trent Bridge was very much to the fore when Nottinghamshire City Council and the other local authorities were considering Nottinghamshire's application for funding in 2007. If it were under threat, it was argued, the economic impact on the region would be enormous, especially with the city's social problems already attracting negative media publicity. The local authorities estimated Trent Bridge's economic value to the city and region at £36 million minimum over 15 years. Hotel occupancy, for example, is at around 95 per cent during Test matches, compared with approximately 60 per cent at other times. They also took into account the contribution that Test match status made to the region's reputation as a centre for sporting excellence by projecting Nottingham to a national and international audience on a regular basis: or as the council's corporate-speak spoke it, 'International events at Trent Bridge are a major showpiece for the city to build reputation and strengthen the city's customer offer as a place to live, work and visit.'

The development work was completed in June 2008, well in time for Trent Bridge to co-host the 2009 ICC World Twenty20 with Lord's, The Oval and Taunton, staging ten games in a fortnight. During the tournament the club and emda commissioned studies to assess the economic impact and media value it generated for the region, and Derek Brewer had more than one reason to be satisfied with the findings. 'We had promised the local press that the benefit would be between £5 million and £10 million. What came out of the studies was an economic impact of around £6.5 million for the East Midlands – £5.7 million of which was spent by visitors from outside the region – and global media exposure valued at £5.7 million. That's £12.2 million in all.'

It was thought that more than 400 million people around the world watched the World Twenty20, with significant coverage in Australia, Europe, India and North America. And while Brewer was able to reflect that his survival strategy for Trent Bridge was achieving its purpose, the Development Agency too could look back on their well-timed assistance. 'The World Twenty20 was just the first return on our investment to help Trent Bridge maintain and grow its status as a world-class venue for cricket and other sports,' said emda's chief executive, Jeff Moores. 'It has already repaid it more than twice over in terms of the economic benefit alone.'

Which is all well and good. But there can be more to success stories than economic return alone. There can be human rewards as well, as Brewer chose to remember when he ended his review of 2009 in Nottinghamshire's annual report. 'As many of you who attended [the World Twenty20] will have seen, mascots from local schools accompanied each player during the national anthems. Prior to the Australia v Sri Lanka match a young lad with cerebral palsy joined Ricky Ponting, the Australian captain, who, recognising that he was a special child, made a real effort to look after him. As the young lad came off the field he told Tracey Francis [Trent Bridge's Community Sports Trust Manager] that this had been the best day of his life. As a sequel, Tracey discovered that he had slept in his mascot outfit every night for the week after the match.

'It was a poignant reflection and, away from the Balance Sheet with which we are all too frequently occupied, should remind us all what this great club is for and the contribution sport in general and cricket in particular can make to the lives of people in Nottinghamshire.'

CHAPTER SIX
TWO TIMING

So what's with this TSF2 that it crops up whenever ground developments get a mention? It sounds like a catch-22. Comply with it and you end up deeper in debt; fail to comply with it and your ground loses its international status. That could be curtains for a Test match county. Or is it just the fall guy for all the debt? Don't blame me aspirations, Guv; it's that TSF2 what led me on. One thing it's not is R2-D2.

Nor is TSF2 bedtime reading, not even for insomniacs. There's much too much bureau-speak and an awful lot of repetition, or should that be a lot of awful repetition? Lad-lit or chick-lit it's not, for the lads and lasses in their ECB livery. It bares all the hallmarks of a sub-committee. No naked ambition, not an ounce of flesh in sight, not even a dark night of the soul.

As mentioned earlier, it followed TSF1, which was kicking around from 1998 until 2006. In ECB language, TSF2 'superseded' TSF1, which is logical and at the same time illogical in a cricketing sense. Batsman two does not supersede batsman one. Batsman one, depending on his standing with the gods, may be superseded by numbers three to 11, but not by two. There's a case to be made for following TSF1 with TSF3; the real problem comes when making a case for TSF2, although its compilers give it a whirl.

Its purpose, they claim, is three-fold. The first is to communicate the ECB's facility strategy for first-class grounds; the second is to communicate the policy 'concerning the Allocation of Matches for consideration by the Major Match Group who shall independently recommend the allocation of Major Matches'; and the third – I can't quote the gobbledegook again; even plagiarism has its standards – indicates what the grounds require to be rated Category A, B and C.

If it's not an oxymoron, TSF2 is enlightening about ECB thinking, for there's a great deal of emphasis on what it calls Major Matches; in other words Test matches, limited-overs internationals and domestic finals, which are played at Category A and B grounds. These get four landscape pages, whereas Category C grounds, the common or garden county grounds, merit half a page and an occasional mention elsewhere. Category C ground toilets, for example, get only one word, the word toilets, and that as an ancillary service along with emergency treatment rooms for players, officials and spectators. Toilets at Test match grounds, however, warrant approximately 160 words. Does that say something about the relative importance the ECB puts on international cricket and the county game? It certainly says they know what pulls in the people.

If you're male, or a male spectator as TSF2 prefers, you should find one urinal for every 70 of you at a Test match ground, while there's one WC for every 35 female spectators. Word has it you're better off being a woman at Lord's than at St Pancras Eurostar terminal. The men have to make do with one WC for every 600, which seems as good a reason as any to have a boiled egg for breakfast and avoid the lunchtime curry, and the chaps don't do so well on the hand-washing front either. They have to get by with one basin for every 300, whereas the women get one for every 70 of them, and they get mirrors and soap dispensers. Something there for the equal opportunities johnnies to investigate when they have a spare moment. Happily TSF2 closes the gender gap when it comes to the water temperature in the pre-mix taps, specifying 43°C to 45°C for both sexes.

What intrigues me is how they know the number of male and female spectators at Test matches in order to calculate these ratios. I can't believe there's a bladder and bowel barometer for sports venues in some government department, although post-1984 anything is possible, I guess. Just don't get caught short at Canterbury, Cheltenham or Colchester, for none of the aforementioned applies there. And heaven help you if you're watching cricket at an out-ground during the London Olympics. Even Glastonbury decided to take five in 2012 because of the expected run on portable loos.

There's much more to TSF2 than toilets, however, a word incidentally of French origin which only goes to show how serious the ECB are in their efforts to take cricket to a wider audience (did I mention that the female cubicles have to be 100mm wider than the male's?). There's the private viewing area at Test match grounds for the WAGs – that's players' wives and guests, the latter presumably embracing girlfriends, a practice taken all too literally by some of the partners with whom the ECB have been to bed with in recent times. Though only for money, one hastens to add. As Meatloaf put it, certain things you don't do for love. The WAGs' area has to be big enough for 40 people, in contrast to the VIP area, which should have enough space for 100 guests. I couldn't help noticing that the WAGs' area is for 'accommodating' whereas the VIP area is for 'entertaining'. Cricket has always known how to keep people in their place.

This for many of us is out in the fresh air. We hope we'll be among the 95 per cent supposed to have an unrestricted view of the playing area – the press should be so lucky at some grounds – and the 90 per cent who can see the scoreboard (assuming the sun is in the right position for reading the digital info). We'll certainly be in the 75 per cent of seating that has to be available to the public. The other 25 per cent includes those seats that often remain empty for an hour or so after lunch, and to give TSF2 its due that 25 per cent might be higher. Back in the days when Test match gate income was handed over to the TCCB, pooled and distributed around all the counties, the Test match grounds tended to invest in corporate facilities ahead of public facilities. It wasn't just that the corporate spend brought in more money. The host county got to keep it, and this was a bone of contention between the Test match counties, the smaller grounds and the Board. These days the grounds keep the ticket income as well, having already agreed to pay the ECB a fee to stage the match.

That's why improved public facilities have become a must. There's more to it now than putting on a game and expecting people to turn up. Turning up has to be a worthwhile experience for more than the cricket. So TSF2 points the Test match grounds in the right direction. Those not in the 25 per cent of seating that has to be covered can be assured that the ground 'will have incorporated the need for rain and sun protection for spectators'. Did R2-D2 ever do as much for humankind? And should it rain, or when it rains, this being England (or Wales), there should be a 'covered facility' away from the spectator's seat where a wise management, it's suggested, will have a 'site for merchandising purposes'. Nothing so vulgar as a shop; Test cricket has gone into retail therapy. Should you feel like a cup of tea and a bath bun, or a plastic pint with a cheese and Branston baguette, rest assured you won't have to 'travel more than 75 metres to the nearest catering facility'. True, this could often be at least five metres further than the minimum that third man is required to amble from his boundary to the wicket when the captain calls on him to bowl. After he's had his gulp of energy drink, of course.

Better to swing a job in the media. They have 'dedicated' toilets for a start. This toilet is dedicated to Sir Ian Botham. This toilet is dedicated to Michael Atherton, OBE. And they usually get to have the best seats in the house, being ostensibly behind (or in front of) the bowler's arm, and they have TV monitors in case they happen to be distracted when something of interest happens, as indeed it sometimes does. The press box has to be tiered with room for 100 journalists at Category A and B grounds – and they get free Internet access to boot. It's suggested this should be monitored in case of inappropriate use. As if!

All this for half a dozen days a year of major match cricket basically. When Yorkshire played Kent at Headingley at the end of 2010, in what was a decisive match for both counties – Yorkshire chasing the Championship title, Kent trying to avoid relegation – the state-of-the-art dual-use press box was closed and the journos were down the hall in a box that resembled a room. They were, however, better off than the scorers and scoreboard operators: they were in a box that, with four people, computers and wires, looked more like the flight deck of a 737. But that's what happens when a ground is Category A one day and, to all intents and purposes, becomes Category C the next. Suddenly it doesn't need media accommodation for 100 people and its minimum public seating requirement is only 3,000, which can be either permanent or temporary.

As for covered seating, don't rely on it. It's not compulsory and it's taken some grounds a century to appreciate that weather protection could be a consumer-conscious asset. There might be a good reason why the traditional county supporter, cocooned in woolly hat, anorak and travelling rug, is supposedly a species in decline.

TSF2 does warn counties to be realistic about being awarded major matches and advises them not to overspend on ground improvements and new facilities. But when you've been a Test match ground for a century or more, you're unlikely to lower your sights, not to mention your members' expectations of international cricket. You bite the bullet, recognise the importance of a business plan that provides income from more than cricket, and you beg or borrow to upgrade your ground appropriately, not only to comply with TSF2 but to attract new and regular commercial business to your facilities.

When TSF2 replaced TSF1, the need to improve grounds was by no means restricted to the Test match venues. Many of the county grounds had dragged themselves into the 21st century looking decidedly down at heel and needing more than the customary off-season lick of paint. They gave the impression that county cricket itself was down at heel, at best a refuge for the retired, a pastime for pensioners. There was a distinct absence of youth, even unemployed youth. If you were lucky enough to spot an attractive young lady you could be pretty certain she'd soon be approaching you with the beneficiary's begging bowl or a clutch of raffle tickets. It wasn't Glastonbury, it wasn't Reading, heaven help us at some places it wasn't even Leyton Orient.

At Chelmsford, a crow's flight north-east of Leyton, David East had long been aware of the need to breathe new life into the Essex county ground. The facilities at New Writtle Street had been recently improved when he first played there in the early 1980s. But, as he said, '30 years later those same facilities are 30 years older and they're dying. Expectations have moved on in terms of quality and of what's required by legislation. In many ways the ground has been struggling to meet the requirement and it was obvious that something had to happen.'

Faced with this reality, the club put together proposals for a major redevelopment of the ground. Whereas many of the previous improvements had been done piecemeal as and when the club could afford it, the result being a rather disjointed infrastructure, Essex now drew up a master plan for a multi-use ground that would provide both modern cricketing facilities and the *de rigueur* capability for banqueting and conferencing. The design included a new entrance piazza, a new bridge to the ground over the River Can and a pathway development including a new media centre. Its projected cost was around £15 million, funded by the club's share of an enabling development for flats on land that Essex were releasing to their development partner.

Somerset had done something similar at Taunton, leasing land at the River Tone end so that Pegasus Homes, a care-home provider, could build retirement flats. 'We've retained the long-term lease on the entire building,' Richard Gould explained, 'so it comes back to the club in 127 years. That might seem a long while away but we've been around since 1875 so we can afford to plan long term.'

It means the club is earning ground rent, and in addition they own something like 5,000 square feet of retail space below the flats. This has been rented out, initially to a cycle shop and to an Italian delicatessen/café with access from inside the ground as well as from the riverfront. Taunton has always been a friendly, welcoming ground, and by utilising the riverfront it's becoming suspiciously chic. Somerset's balance sheet also took on an upbeat aspect, helped not just by the sale of the lease for the flats but also by the new permanent seating in front of them. Increased ground capacity in 2009 was measured in increased gate receipts of more than 50 per cent.

Gould was particularly pleased with one feature of the Taunton development which in itself was not a revenue earner. Not directly, anyway. 'We've put a gap between the Botham and Trescothick Stands to give people on the river path visibility into the ground. With the stand that was there before you didn't necessarily know what was happening on the other side. I want people during a Championship match to be going up the steps and peeking in through the bars of the gate. It's another way of creating a bit more interest in the club. One day they might want to come in. Also it adds something to Taunton as you're walking beside the river, which is cool.'

What Essex add to Chelmsford eventually played out in their favour during the protracted planning process that preceded permission for their redevelopment plans. At the start the local authority was not entirely supportive, and it took a change of administration to bring about a change of heart. Then as late as 2009 the planning application was called in for a public enquiry to resolve a standing objection from the Environment Agency. Part of the development was on land considered a flood plain, and it was well into 2010 before Essex were given the go-ahead.

'One of the proposals we looked at early on was to move to the outskirts of Chelmsford,' East said. 'The council were very much against that, however. They see the club as an integral, integrated part of the central Chelmsford leisure offer. They consider the revenue, focus and attention we bring are very important to the town. In fact it formed a significant part of the economic impact assessment they did on our behalf when our planning application was called in by the Secretary of State.'

While compliance with TSF1/2 was a major factor in their need to improve the ground's facilities, Essex were also conscious of another, more long-term benefit to be gained from their development plans.

'We'd like to think that part of our objective is to reduce our reliance on ECB central funds. The more autonomous we can become, the greater flexibility we'll have in terms of coping with ECB funding fluctuations in the years ahead. In an ideal world you'd want to be in a position where the ECB money was the icing on the cake, where our cricket was funded exclusively by ECB activities while the commercial and marketing activities serviced the club. That would be great but we're not there yet, and I suspect we won't be for some time.'

What never featured in the Essex game plan, however, was international cricket. Unlike one or two of the non-Test match grounds, they were never sucked (or suckered) into the belief that one day Chelmsford could be a venue for one-day and Twenty20 internationals. What Paul Millman, a tad derisively, calls the sexy side of the game. David East explained why. 'When you look at the constraints our site has in terms of seating capacity, we're realistic about what we can stage. In a way the decision's been taken out of our hands. We can be pragmatic about it. But even if the rules were to change, would we want to do it? We've got Lord's and The Oval down the road and any reasonable person is going to go to one of them for international cricket. Our lines of communication in and out of London are so good, and those two venues have the capacity that gives international cricket such a great atmosphere.

'The chances of us aspiring to stage international cricket and being successful are very limited, so why have a stadium for it that's going to be vacant a lot of the time? Our focus is on domestic cricket: Twenty20 using the floodlights, a tourist game against the county, England Lions, things like that.'

It's a philosophy, a realism that almost half the first-class counties subscribe to. These are the eight Category C grounds: Derbyshire, Essex, Kent, Leicestershire, Northamptonshire, Somerset, Sussex and Worcestershire. Not that all of them buy into the need for permanent floodlights, in spite of TSF2's exhortations and the ECB's financial incentives: £100,000 over five years in performance-related payments for domestic-standard floodlights and £500,000 over the same period for international-standard lights. The standard is determined by the lux level of the lights – the degree of illumination at the batting crease, within the fielding circle and, for international standard, on the boundary. As for what decides the need for floodlights, television is as much a consideration as spectator appeal. The ECB might pooh-pooh the suggestion, but TSF2 gives the game away by obliging counties to play at least one game a season under lights – if so required by the Board 'to fulfil the terms of the current broadcasting agreement'.

Somerset is one county that has no time for floodlights. They prefer to stage their games in good evening light at a family-friendly time. And at Leicester's Grace Road, David Smith wasn't convinced either that floodlights had a great deal to offer commercially. 'At the height of summer, where we've pushed our Twenty20 games to, we're light until 9.30 to 10 so the lights have no impact. Whereas the times they come into their own, May, late August and September, it's also cold.'

It certainly can be, as Somerset's Vic Marks noted in the *Guardian* after a poorly attended floodlit Twenty20 international at Cardiff in early September 2010. 'The crowd,' he wrote with some heartfelt sympathy, 'huddled near the floodlights as much for warmth as light. Floodlit cricket in England [and Wales] in September requires a strong constitution and a high-quality anorak.'

Maybe the floodlight experience will gather speed with global warming but when 2010's Twenty20 season hit off in June you knew from the goosebumps on the go-go dancers' flesh that you were in Sussex by the sea and not Sydney or Cape Town. The pies were a give-away, too, but that's another matter altogether and one not covered by TSF2.

The question of whether grounds have floodlights or not is one of those areas which differentiate the 18 counties' business models. They further emphasise the juggling act that the ECB have to perform when planning a playing schedule that suits all of them. A domestic Twenty20 competition boxed into a midsummer block obviously suits those counties who haven't felt the need to invest in floodlights. But what if someone were to come along with the ambition and the finance for a floodlit tournament spread across the season? Or late in the season? Temporary floodlights might suffice to satisfy current broadcasting demands, but there's surely a limit to the number of times counties could have trucks trundling in and out of their grounds.

Approaching Northamptonshire's county ground after some ten years absence I was surprised to see floodlight pylons towering over the neighbourhood chimney pots. They'd once been a feature (if that's the right word) when the Northampton Town football ground adjoined the cricket ground, but that was back in the long-gone days of Cooks and Capel, Larkins and Lamb. The Cobblers had been gone since 1994 and an impressive cricket centre with indoor nets now adorned the Abington Avenue entrance.

The floodlights were impressive as well, throwing out more illumination than TSF2 requires for Category A and B grounds. Planning permission can't have been all that straightforward, and chief executive Mark Tagg agreed that they did have a lengthy battle against well-organised local opposition before winning approval. There are certainly some attractive houses with big gardens to one side of the ground and no doubt some owners were as concerned about the impact on property values as they were about intrusion from the lights and the noise of night-time cricket.

'The planning permission says we can turn them on 15 times,' said Tagg. 'The first season we had them on seven nights, plus practice. That was five Twenty20s and two CB40s, four on Friday nights. I'd like to have a maximum of ten matches, with a tourist game if that was a one-day game and hold one back for a home quarter-final or a semi in a knockout stage. Floodlit cricket enables us to play at the right time of day for our Northants fans, besides which I don't like missing out on ECB investment if there's money to be had. If they're going to give me half a million pounds for some lights I'm going to take it.'

Northampton is one of those small county grounds that can leave you fearful for the future of county cricket one day and convinced of its survival the next. A full house is 5,000 seated and 1,000 standing, although standing room only isn't a problem according to Tagg. 'Northampton people don't tend to mind standing short-term because they're used to it at the Saints and the Cobblers, where they've got a lot of standing. Even if you've got enough seats, you'll find partway through the game that some seats are empty because people prefer to stand by the bar or over at the hotdog stand or wherever and have a natter.'

When I stopped going to county cricket regularly it was the natter I missed most, so I was pleased to hear that it hadn't lost its place. I got into one with a policewoman the next time I went to Northampton. They get prettier as well as younger the older you get, and the natter took my mind off the cricket. It was all sixes and fours and funny noises over the PA system whenever there was a bowling change. Somehow the game ended in a tie and we all went home happy in our different ways.

If their six floodlight pylons can be said to represent Northamptonshire's ambitions for a brighter future, there is some serious backroom planning at play as well. Tagg, like David East at Essex, is all too aware that they and all the counties are completely dependent on their ECB money. 'We couldn't survive without it. But going forward the business plan for all counties has to be to generate more revenue themselves. We've been very tight on costs, and we continue to be, but driving external revenue is the way forward. Things like tribute nights, networking lunches and outdoor cinema evenings. When we have the big replay screen in for one of our TV games, we negotiate with the big-screen guys to keep it here for another 24 hours and we sell the next evening as a bring your picnic supper and watch a classic film or whatever.'

The tribute nights – Abba Gold, Take That 2, that kind of thing – are held in the indoor cricket centre and come complete with a meal. The success of commercial activities like this have led to some interesting conflicts of interest, not least because the indoor centre is first and foremost a cricket facility. Or that's how Northants head coach David Capel sees it. The commercial department take a different viewpoint. 'So now I have David saying, Look, I need to know when it's available for cricket,' Mark Tagg laughed.

At a time when consumer spending is tighter than it has been for many years, Northamptonshire have shown courage as well as initiative by investing in the commercial side of their business when other counties were cutting back on theirs, either not replacing people or even making redundancies. Tagg thought the club had their biggest commercial department ever. 'It's a much more professional sell now. It's not the traditional cricket sell. People have been saying, "This is a bit different for Northants". But it works. We've shown that if you get the right people selling and you can supply the right product, a nice sponsors' lounge for meals, good quality food, you can still sell. We've even been taking business from the Saints and the Cobblers.'

Northants Cricket, as they brand themselves, might not be able to match the rugby and the football when it comes to numbers through the gates, but they've learnt what it takes to sell tables. 'We have to be positive,' Tagg continued, 'whatever the economic situation in the country. We've made the investment in lights, we've had the car park resurfaced, we've done some tarting up around the ground, so we've stacked money into the club and we have to make it pay. The franchise argument? We don't want to be there. We want to be significant as Northants Cricket, that's our vision, to be the best county ground or cricket club. Not Test match, not one-day international but county cricket.'

This is the county that in 2008 were fielding half a dozen players not qualified for England, mostly South Africans. No one in their Championship team had been born in Northamptonshire. 'It was awful,' Tagg admitted. 'Behind the scenes we all knew it was awful and we had to deal with it.' A few years before that, their South

African director of cricket, Kepler Wessels, had been quoted as saying the reason the county played so many non-England qualified players was because the local leagues weren't good enough to provide English ones. 'That went down like a lead balloon,' Tagg remembered with a grimace.

Things changed, not least because the ECB's Player Related Performance Fee (PRPF) payments have helped concentrate minds when it comes to counties employing non-England qualified players. The PRPFs reward counties for bringing on young English players and producing England cricketers. Consequently, when the ECB remunerate counties each time one of their players represents England in a Test match, one-day international or Twenty20 international, or goes on an overseas tour, that payment might be divided between the player's current county and his previous county or counties according to his time there as an academy, age-group or registered cricketer. While England spinners Graeme Swann and Monty Panesar no longer play for Northamptonshire, for example, they have nonetheless continued to provide a financial payback for the county that developed them.

'If Swanny breaks a leg tomorrow,' Tagg admitted, 'I've lost £100,000. That's big money for a county this size.'

Lessons learnt, Northamptonshire set about providing a development pathway that would lead the county's young cricketers to the county ground, working with their Cricket Board to involve all the local districts and age-group managers. Their aim was to ensure that the Northants cricket community understood what the county club were trying to do. 'We've now got a proper route by which the parents of an eight-year-old can see what's happening year on year regarding their lad or lass. And we aim to get the coaches of our age-group and district teams up to Level 3.'

That's the vision: the best coaching set-up for the best youngsters across Northamptonshire to produce cricketers for the county's emerging players squads, for their academy, for their county side and ultimately for England. The best strength and conditioning programme, the best pitches to play on. And if their young players then go off to play for a larger county? 'It's inevitable. If we can get two, three years of those kids being successful for us, that's fine. It'd be great to have an England side with Notts and Warwickshire players who started off at Northants. I'd be proud of that,' says Tagg.

Consequently the cricket features strongly behind the boundary at Northampton. Tagg's aim when I spoke to him in 2010 was to enhance the Wantage Road side of the ground – 'Not redevelop but enhance,' he emphasised – to provide three changing rooms, two physiotherapy suites, a strategy room and a gym that would serve both players and the public. There were also plans for a fitness studio for public use.

'It's all about providing the best we can for young players in particular, and for their parents. If they're given the choice of going to Essex, Derby, Leicester or Northants, we may not be able to pay the top dollar but the parents will know their kids are getting the best facilities, the best coaching and they'll be able to play for Northamptonshire and go on hopefully to play for England. That's our niche, that's where we can deliver. That's how we can be valuable to the Team England ethos. And that's how we'll survive. By producing cricketers for England.'

If any of these young Northants cricketers turn out to be the next generation's Graeme Swann or Monty Panesar, England and their army of supporters won't mind at all.

CHAPTER SEVEN
UNINTENDED CONSEQUENCES

Out of all the euphoria that accompanied Cardiff's debut Test match – England's great escape that set the scene for the gripping 2009 Ashes series – *Wisden Cricketers' Almanack* pulled a few rabbits from the statistical top hat. 'With 1,700 temporary catering staff serving 152,000 pints of beer and supplying 12,500 bacon rolls from mostly Welsh suppliers,' wrote its Glamorgan correspondent, Edward Bevan, 'conservative estimates indicated that the Welsh economy was boosted by £20 million as a direct result of the game.' Now that's what you call an economic impact study.

Glamorgan's annual accounts put the turnover from the Test at £5.8 million, against which were set £4.98 million in costs including a reported £3.2 million bid fee to the ECB. The size and the provenance of the Glamorgan bid were the focus of grumbling by Test match counties on the other side of the Severn, and it didn't help English sensibilities that two Welshmen, ECB chairman David Morgan and Glamorgan chairman Paul Russell, were on the ECB board of directors when Cardiff was awarded the Test match ahead of Durham, Hampshire and Lancashire. But there were few complaints, if any, from those fortunate enough to witness the game at Test cricket's hundredth venue. The club, the city and the Principality had every reason to bask in the congratulations that came their way in the days that followed.

Since being allocated their Ashes Test in April 2006, Glamorgan had spent more than £15 million rebuilding the Sophia Gardens ground. It was more than a rebuild really. It was a dream become reality, an ambition transformed into a 16,000 capacity stadium with naming rights sold to South Wales Electricity (SWALEC) for £1.5 million. And yet in spite of the resounding success it is nonetheless instructive that the ground was not sold out for every day of the Ashes Test. The club blamed the UK's recession for their failure to sell as much hospitality as they originally anticipated, and their budget suffered a different kind of hit from the economic downturn when interest rates dropped. Having sold a large proportion of the Test tickets by the end of 2008, and with their bid fee not payable until 30 days after the match finished, Glamorgan had some £2.4 million in hand. They had hoped to cash in by investing the money short-term in a Treasury reserve account, only to see their anticipated return drop to around one per cent as the Bank of England (but not of Wales) cut interest rates. There were no swings and roundabouts either. Most of their borrowings to develop the ground were at fixed interest rates, costing the club £536,111 in 2008 and £605,845 in 2009. All in all they must have been pinching themselves when the numbers for 2009 were eventually crunched and came up with a pre-tax profit of £338,324. Turnover had increased by 71 per cent, thanks mostly to the Test match, and the operating profit was up 57 per cent.

But, as on the other side of the Second Severn Crossing, there was a reality check in store come 2010. Cardiff's three internationals – a floodlit one-dayer in June and two Twenty20s in three days in September – managed to attract only 31,154 in total, with the meagre 5,691 turnout for the second Twenty20 sending shivers down many spines. Even if there were extenuating circumstances, not least Vic Marks's chilly Cardiff night, it did go to show, as Abraham Lincoln might have said, you can fill all the grounds some of the time, and some of the grounds all the time, but you cannot fill all the grounds all the time. Not when the number of grounds had increased at the same time as the standard of international cricket had become alarmingly variable.

To quote the other newcomer to the international arena, the Rose Bowl's Rod Bransgrove, 'There's too much ordinary cricket. In my opinion it's devaluing the sovereignty of Test match cricket. We should never devalue how great Test cricket should be. If you've ever sat in a dressing room after a great Test match and seen how much it matters after five days of mental and physical battle, you would recognise the huge impact on the players. But the people in charge don't talk about it like that. They talk about it as being a great saleable commodity, arguing that you will earn more by playing more. This is analogous to an argument for playing the FIFA World Cup every year, twice a year, simply because it is the most lucrative sporting event on Earth. It is the rarity value, however, that creates the value. Test matches are fantastic competitions, played properly. Wonderful, wonderful. And they should be rare.'

So how come we're getting so many, and so many grounds want to stage them? Money is the obvious answer, to which should be added the conditions of the ECB's television contracts with Sky. In recent years the maximum number of Tests in a season has been seven, although this increased to eight in 2010 when England became the surrogate venue for two Test matches between Australia and Pakistan. For many years, up until 2000, there were six Tests a summer, while the days of five Tests and zero one-day internationals are more than 40 years ago, in an era when Geoffrey Boycott and Ian Chappell were batting instead of blathering, scoring runs rather than points as media gurus.

Former Leicestershire chairman Neil Davidson shares Bransgrove's fear that Test cricket is being devalued at the very time it needs to be made special again. Listening to the two men's views, it's hardly surprising that they have not always been the most welcome of voices at ECB meetings. Yet they are not alone in their concerns. Others, too, are troubled that the response to cricket's financial problems has too often been to throw in more 'product'.

'There's a danger in not drawing a distinction between the number of games and the value of the games,' said Durham's David Harker. 'If the audience isn't there, or there hasn't been the investment to develop that audience, you can have as many games as you like but you're not going to make any money if nobody's watching them.'

It's the age-old dichotomy of upping the supply side at the risk of diminishing the demand. 'The ECB are responding to the belief that the grounds want more games. No. What we want are more attractive games that the whole of cricket can benefit from. I'd be happy to have less international cricket at Chester-le-Street if the cricket I have is sold out.'

Generally speaking there is not much sympathy for the Test match grounds from the smaller counties. Their over-riding opinion is that going to nine international grounds was just plain wrong because the ECB cannot give that many grounds enough Test matches and international cricket to service their debts. But David East, looking at the bigger picture, had some sympathy for the Test match grounds and their predicament. 'We can't operate without the international grounds,' was how he saw it. 'We need them to be vibrant and successful so that the whole game can benefit from that. With all the will in the world I can't get 16,000 people in our ground to stage a Test match, so we do need those venues. But going from seven to nine grounds with seven Test matches doesn't work and there are clubs that are hurting. They've got themselves into a muddle. They've seen staging international cricket as a holy grail, as a cash cow, and that would be fine if you didn't have new entrants. It's something I remember from my business strategy days. If you don't allow for new entrants coming into the market you've got the potential for a failed business plan.'

Richard Gould had no doubt that there was going to be some pain on the way for some clubs. But, as he said, 'It's the same for anyone making an investment. They knew what the risks were, and it's not as if it's a market where you can't see what everybody else is doing. If a county has come up with an unsustainable model, who should bear the pain for that? The other 17 counties or the county's investors?'

His chairman at Somerset, Andy Nash, was even more pragmatic. 'Speaking as a businessman I think there's a very grown-up answer, which is that the creditors have made the wrong call and they should pay the bill. I'm very clear that members of the ECB are not going to bail out any county that's got itself into a debt level it can't service.'

Paul Millman wasn't surprised that Nash took the line he did. The two had worked together at Merrydown when Nash came in as chairman of the cider-maker. He respected him as a tough but fair-minded businessman, but he'd been in cricket administration longer and he saw another side of the over-capacity dilemma. He knew from his own experience at Kent that some counties had been led into thinking they could become major match grounds if they had the right facilities. The carrot had been dangled. It wasn't simply a case of imprudent management or, as some critics claimed, over-ambition, ego or the desire to uphold a tradition.

'Following the 1999 World Cup,' he told Nash, 'several of us got excited about staging international cricket. We started thinking, hey, we could become an international ground, and at the time there were people at the ECB wanting to cut into the old Test match grounds' dominance. I went to Lord's and sat with Rod Bransgrove as sort of aspirational international grounds and we were given the big come-on. No doubt about it, and we started to build our plans on that aspiration. It should have been possible to look at the international programme going forward and to see it was unrealistic for us; that we had no part to play in it, that there were too many grounds chasing the same dream. But there was no strategic capacity plan. No one had done a capacity analysis, a facilities matrix if you like that says cricket needs only X number of international grounds.'

Andy Nash was having none of it. 'If you allowed yourself to be teased along, then I'm afraid ultimately you're culpable for where you end up. You have to be responsible for your own destiny. We too have had the same level of encouragement in the past to go down the international route, and we resisted it. We were encouraged to get into property speculation when the Somerset Stand went up, and we resisted that. I'm not saying we get it right all the time. All I'm saying is that you have to live with the consequences of your decisions. I'm afraid the TMGs, whether they were led or whether they went there of their own volition, have clearly ended up in a place that appears to be economically unviable.

'But that's not the end of the story, because Yorkshire can very easily go bust tomorrow and a phoenix can rise within 24 hours, minus the debts of the creditors. It's a perfectly viable cricket ground and will continue to be. There will always be cricket played at Headingley. All of this debate is about how the creditors are going to share the pain. There is overwhelming precedent for how that can be easily sorted out. Very painful for the creditors, accepted, but it can be sorted out in 24 hours.'

About the same time there were economists at that other ECB, the European Central Bank, wondering if the same conclusion could be reached about such countries as Greece, Ireland and Portugal, to name just three whose debt levels were causing jitters in the financial markets. It can be a harsh old world out there, and cricket has no right to presume it's immune to its realities. It has nothing to lose but its reputation for fair play.

We might wonder why our ECB, as English cricket's governing body, didn't take on board the potential for crisis. But didn't we all wonder where governments and the appropriate regulatory bodies were prior to what down under they call the North Atlantic economic crisis? Most counties will admit that there is a lack of leadership from the ECB when it comes to them, but with their next breath they will defend each county's prerogative to set its own agenda, run its own business plan, decide its own destiny. It reminded me of something I'd been reading on one of my train journeys, an article in *Prospect* magazine by Richard Price, an old boy, I believe, of Jonathan Agnew and Stephen Fry's alma mater, Uppingham. Price, however, had made his name as an international investor rather than an entertainer and tweeter. 'In any successful business with 17 divisions,' he'd written, 'you'll get 17 managing directors. Not all will move at the same pace. Inevitably, the bigger you get, one or two will fail.'

And as a few chief executives with miles on the clock told me, 'The ECB will be quite happy for a few of us to go out of business.'

Richard Gould agreed with Millman that a better-structured administration would have led the counties away from a perilous situation instead of into one. But along with his county chairman he believed nonetheless that counties that chose to invest heavily in international cricket 'ultimately are the ones that need to live or die by their own business plans.'

As for why the ECB didn't rein in counties whose ambitions went beyond their means, their defence could be that they are only the servants of the counties and so lacked the authority to stop them. Ask why there was no clear strategic plan for international cricket, rather than one dictated by television, and they could say with some justification that they hadn't foreseen the scarcity of quality international cricket, or the emergence of the IPL as a potential competitor to international cricket. They are only suits and blazers after all, not soothsayers or Sibyls. Just Basils.

And, as economists and politicians like to remind us, there is something called the Law of Unintended Consequences. It has several definitions but they boil down to something similar, more or less. A policy, a decision, an action can have an unexpected negative effect in addition to the desired one. We are where we are because of where we've been, as someone must have said some time or another, if only George W. Bush or one of his motley crew.

A few lines in *Wisden* 2000, the Millennium Edition, set me thinking about the Law of Unintended Consequences. Down at the back of the book, in the steerage class section called Meetings and Decisions in 1999, it was noted that, 'A meeting of the First-Class Forum on 31 March was unable to conclude financial negotiations with the Test Match Grounds Consortium, representing those counties who stage matches and were seeking a larger share of ECB profits in recompense.' There was also mention of a discussion on plans for a 25-over evening league, but we know what became of those. To find out what became of the Test Match Grounds Consortium and their negotiations, I went to see Tim Lamb. All of this may have happened in another century but it happened nevertheless on his watch.

'We did get caught up in a bit of a crisis,' he recalled, the intervening length of time or a certain kind of English composure underplaying the possible seriousness of the situation. Maybe it was a bit of both. Tim Lamb had his critics when he was chief executive of the ECB, but he was a good man to be on the wrong side of. He had a sense of perspective, he never forgot his manners; he understood that, even in opposition, you were both doing your job and that was not something you had to fall out over. Not for life anyway.

'The Test match grounds formed themselves into a cartel and more or less held a gun to the ECB's head, basically saying that, unless there was an improvement in the terms and conditions under which international matches were staged, the grounds might break away or prevent us from staging matches with them. We actually went so far as carrying out an analysis of the financial consequences if we had to play Test matches at non-Test match grounds. We had to do it in case the Test match grounds were serious with what they were threatening.'

Behind the scenes the dispute was just another sore in the festering saga between the big markets and the small ones. This time the catalyst was the amount of money the major match grounds were or weren't making from staging international games. 'There were absolutely polarised opinions between, say, the Surreys and Warwickshires of this world and the Leicestershires and Derbyshires. The Surreys and Warwickshires would say, "Of course we make a lot of money and it's all transparent, it's in our accounts. We need it to invest in the infrastructure of our grounds, to provide better facilities for the ECB to stage matches and generate money through broadcasting rights, through commercial income and so on." At the same time some of the non-TMGs were saying, "Look, we understand we have to accept that the TMGs stage international cricket because we haven't got the facilities or the capacity to do so. But in return we expect the TMGs to play fair. While we understand that they need to generate more money to improve their stadiums, why should they have more money to spend on players?" Which, of course, the TMGs denied and pointed to other counties like Kent who were reportedly paying equally as much as the Surreys of this world in players' salaries, and probably finding ways around the thing by giving other incentives as well.'

Peter Edwards, secretary/general manager of Essex until his sudden death in 2000, had strong views on the subject of the Test match grounds and their accounting practices. Listening to Tim Lamb brought back memories of some interesting, probably slanderous, conversations with Peter over pre-match coffees at Chelmsford. 'Feisty' could have been given its modern usage in order to describe him, especially when it came to his championing of three-day county cricket. In fact he did more than just champion it. In the same way that his successor, David East, has made money out of Twenty20 at a time when other counties were losing money or their nerve, Peter Edwards made money out of the old-style Championship by ensuring that Essex played a brand of cricket that people would pay to see. During his time on the ECB management board, his *Wisden* obituary noted, 'He was painted by Lord's officials as a reactionary, which was a … nonsense.'

More reactionary in fact was the decision of the Test match grounds, prompted particularly by MCC and Warwickshire, to set up their cartel, the self-styled Test Match Grounds Consortium, to protect their own interests. Self-interest is a constant motivator among the counties, if my travels around the grounds are anything to go by, so things must have come to a pretty pass to get six established Test match counties to strike up a consortium.

What was happening was Durham's emergence in the north-east, not only as the 18th first-class county but as a prospective international ground. The writing was on the wall. Where one county led, there was the chance that others would follow. That would mean fewer major matches to share around and, just as serious for the six Test match grounds, it would weaken their negotiating position with the ECB. Here's Tim Lamb again. 'One of the reasons we felt it necessary to look outside the traditional six grounds is that there were some, when it came to Test match cricket, who we didn't think were pulling their weight when it came to promoting ticket sales. Whereas the Test match grounds retained the income from corporate hospitality, ground advertising and other commercial activities they undertook during the course of a Test match, within certain agreed guidelines, the ticketing income came into the ECB, was pooled and the net proceeds were distributed around the whole game as part of the distribution.

'We felt, with the possible exception of games against Australia, which sold themselves really – and these matters were discussed in finance committees and suchlike – that we needed to put some of the TMGs on notice that we were not satisfied with their performance. They somehow seemed to be looking after the areas where they kept the revenue but they weren't, in our view, pulling their weight when it came to selling tickets of which we were the beneficiaries.

'So that's why the arrival of Durham with their magnificent ground up in Chester-le-Street, and then Hampshire coming to tell us about their ambitions for the Rose Bowl, were a potential opportunity for the ECB because we thought it would introduce some much needed competition. And that, of course, was another factor in the formation of the Test Match Grounds Consortium, because they felt that their traditional position was being challenged by the ECB and some of the other counties.'

The upshot of all this was the MCC secretary, Roger Knight, taking a walk around Lord's to the offices of his tenant, the ECB, and personally handing Tim Lamb a letter containing the consortium's terms for staging international cricket. Actually he handed over a brown envelope, Lamb thought, accepted the offer of a cup of tea and sat down to explain what was in the letter. Because, this being cricket, and this being Lord's, that was how things were done among cricket people, especially cricket people with the background that Knight and Lamb shared: public schools, Oxbridge, county cricket and MCC membership. MCC people may have regarded Tim Lamb as something of a dangerous radical with his modern ideas on marketing cricket, but like Roger Knight he was establishment through and through. Whether it's like that at Lord's today is another matter.

It is perhaps not surprising that the ECB and the Test match grounds negotiated themselves out of confrontation and reached an accommodation. The result of the Test match grounds' strong-arm tactics was the introduction of staging agreements, which gave them the certainty of Test match cricket that they were looking for.

'There'll always be some argument as to whether we conceded too much ground or we didn't,' Lamb said, 'but in the final analysis an agreed position was arrived at, it was approved by the first-class counties (albeit with some reluctance) and the staging agreements were signed. Not everybody was happy with them. Some people felt that they worked too much in favour of the Test match grounds, some people felt they worked too much in favour of the ECB, but at least more certainty and transparency were brought to the process.'

Whatever certainty the staging agreements brought, it didn't last long. It went out of the window with the introduction of the bid process which, by 2010, would have the Test match counties up in arms again, except by now there were nine of them rather than six and there was no brown envelope being walked around Lord's. Instead, the Test match grounds commissioned accountants Deloitte to carry out a root-and-branch review of their finances and the perilous state of the county game's economy. All that the staging agreements had achieved was breathing space for the ECB; time for them to shore up their defences and get the non-Test match counties onside against future mutinies. As stand-offs go it had not been a standout success for the major grounds once the short-term had elapsed. Ten years after, they were at each other's throats rather than the ECB's, desperate to outbid each other to get their next match. If they'd ever been a cosy little unit, they were not that any more.

The days of the consortium felt much more than a decade ago. Intentionally or not the ECB, by bringing in the bid process, had shown themselves remarkably adept at divide-and-rule tactics. It was perhaps another unintended consequence of that letter in the brown envelope.

CHAPTER EIGHT
NEW KIDS ON THE BLOCK

There's a case to be made for arguing that the Test match counties would be in less of a pickle now if they'd got on with improving their grounds ten or so years ago. Instead, the argument would run, they sat back on their staging agreements rather than investing in better facilities. There were a few exceptions, notably Lord's and The Oval, but by failing to follow their example the other grounds basically left a vacuum. They say that nature hates a vacuum; at least that's what the character Brick says to his father, Big Daddy, in Tennessee Williams's play, *Cat on a Hot Tin Roof*. And there's doubtless some truth in it, because whenever there's a vacuum someone or something inevitably comes along to fill it. In the instance of the Test match grounds, that something was the Rose Bowl. That someone was Rod Bransgrove. Since he saved Hampshire from oblivion and turned the Rose Bowl from potential white elephant into the elephant in the ECB's committee rooms, there have likely been those who would go along with Big Daddy's response. 'That's what they say, but sometimes I think that a vacuum is a hell of a lot better than some of the stuff nature replaces it with.'

Bransgrove is the first to admit that he's not a committee man. It's his view that committees have long been one of cricket's problems. I'd go along with that, if for no better reason than I've ridden both a horse and a camel. 'With all respect to some very nice people,' he says, 'it's difficult for well intentioned, well meaning people all to get together and try to run what's become a professional business. That's why, when I came into Hampshire, I restructured it as a plc with a board of directors, and with the ground separate from the cricket club. It doesn't take very long to recognise that domestic cricket is not a commercially viable business. It doesn't have a commercially viable product.'

Nor does it take too long in Bransgrove's company to recognise that he is passionate about Hampshire County Cricket Club and the ground he took on in 2000. His wife laughingly refers to the Rose Bowl as his allotment because he is always down there tinkering. I'd say it was more than tinkering. Bransgrove, solidly built with a workman's hands, may not be a builder by trade but he is by nature. This is a man who is driven not by success alone but by the desire to make things work. He gets things done.

The day I met his wife, at the allotment naturally, she was in discussion with a party planner just in from LA: they were putting together a party for Bransgrove's 60th birthday. It had the makings of a swell affair. The two women had been dancers together in the London run of *42nd Street*: tall, slim and leggy like a few of the women in Team Bransgrove. No airs but plenty of grace. Well, if someone were going to get cricket out of the pages of *Wisden* and into *Rolling Stone*, Rod Bransgrove would be the man. He's no dyed-in-the-wool traditionalist, that's for sure, although he would argue that he does appreciate and enjoy the traditions of sport. His detractors, of whom there's no shortage among the cricket hierarchy, would claim he doesn't, which makes him laugh.

'There's no point in traditionalism just for the sake of it,' he says. 'It's great having the history, but the history should never dictate the future. It has no place there. When people say that Lord's is the home of cricket, I say it's a wonderful place, a wonderful symbol of the game, a record of the history of cricket. But I'm trying to build a ground here that looks to the game's future. I want to have the best modern-day cricket ground we can design and build. At the same time I still pay homage to the heritage of cricket in Hampshire because that has been very important in getting this club to where it is today.'

What Bransgrove doesn't add is that without him the club wouldn't be where it is today. Maybe after a decade he takes it for granted that Hampshire cricket club and the Rose Bowl were always going to be twined in his destiny. The more he talks about the Rose Bowl, the more it becomes obvious that this is more than a cricket ground, and also more than a wealthy man's folly. Only those who only cricket know would see it as that, and sadly for the game, as much as for Bransgrove, there are a few of those about.

As the years passed, and the land where a lone horse grazed grew into an international sports complex with a nine-hole golf course adjoining the cricket ground, it became easy and sometimes conveni-ent to forget that the Rose Bowl was not Rod Bransgrove's baby. He rescued it, fostered it, then adopted it.

When Hampshire decided to move from the old Northlands Road ground, he said, 'They had plans for a workable cricket ground which would have cost in the region of £18 million. But encouraged by Sport England, their funding partner, their aspirations increased and they went to one of the country's top architects, Sir Michael Hopkins, to design a pavilion that would be iconic rather than simply functional. A condition of the funding was that it would be both a domestic and international ground, not many people know that, and so the agenda was already set for me when I came in.'

The early plans certainly made provision for staging international cricket, one-dayers no doubt, by providing wide ledges, or berms, on which to erect temporary stands.

It was quickly apparent to Bransgrove that the Rose Bowl would no longer work as a domestic ground. The bar was already too high. And so were the costs: over budget and escalating. Hampshire County Cricket Club was about to go down the gurgler. Nor were their inaus-picious circumstances merely the result of an over-ambitious build; other miscalculations contributed to their predicament.

'The Northlands Road ground had been sold for development without any sell-on clauses. Typically, what happens to development land is that it gets passed around a few times as people add on value, and each time it's sold the value is that much greater. But Hampshire sold it outright, so as it got further developed there was no additional benefit to the club. Probably the most serious thing that went wrong for them, however, was that they developed the new ground on the assumption they would land a ground-name sponsor who would provide millions of pounds. Those millions never manifested.'

By the time Bransgrove took over the club, they had spent their £18 million and were committed to even more. 'My calculation when I first looked was that they were probably insolvent to the tune of £1.8 million, but as time went on it became much more than that, of course. It became a big headache,' he adds with a chuckle. The way he laughs you wouldn't think he believes that this is the hardest job he's ever done.

'I can remember saying right up top that a capital development project of this size would stretch the boards of directors of major plcs. My management team at the moment are running on fumes, we are all exhausted.'

With new stands either side of the pavilion, and another stand at the opposite end of the bowl-shaped arena, the ground capacity has grown to 25,000. The costs have grown with that. Add on another nine holes to create an 18-hole Championship golf course, throw in a four-star, 175-bedroom hotel that will incorporate hospitality boxes overlooking the ground, and Bransgrove is looking at estimates of between £80 million and £100 million. This is not the cricket ground that Hampshire's committee envisaged when they first leased the land long term from Queen's College, Oxford, and in 1997 watched with much optimism as the constructors broke ground. They probably didn't envisage it as a rock stadium either, pulling in world-renowned groups such as The Who, R.E.M. and Oasis. They might have considered a Neil Diamond concert. Not quite Mark Nicholas in blue jeans but maybe the next best thing for some Hampshire supporters at the time.

The hotel has a starring role in the Rose Bowl infrastructure now, but it wasn't initially integral to Bransgrove's thinking. 'What we did in 2004 was to review our plans for domestic and international cricket, and what would need to be done to make the business model work. I'd actually been forecasting some years ago that the amount of international cricket we play is unsustainable. There's a blindness, a blind spot, in this country. We still think that Test match cricket will sell out seven times a year every year ad infinitum. Well it won't. England against Australia will continue to sell out as long as we don't overplay it. Probably England against India will be an attractive Test match, but others are getting to be a difficult sell now. So my view was, we needed to be looking at other things.

'I gave the project to KPMG and said, here's 115 acres of land and more available if we want it. I want you to look at everything: soccer domes, ski slopes, golf driving ranges, hotels, nurseries, the whole shooting match. And they completed that review for me in 2005. By far the most favourable option was to have an international entertainment venue served by a high-quality hotel, given that we're only one junction away from Southampton airport. We tested it with the local council because we knew we had planning issues. This is supposed to be reserved for outdoor sports and facilitating buildings, but we got through all those kind of things.

'This business model does really work well and I'm quite excited, because what I needed to do was create a business which is sustainable in the long term and which ring-fences Hampshire cricket, insulating it against failure. As long as this business is here, there's a golden share in the constitution of Rose Bowl plc that forces the shareholders to get the agreement of the trustees of Hampshire cricket to anything that may have the effect of first-class cricket not being played here. So if I fell under a bus, as people say, the future of Hampshire cricket is protected, not only in terms of matches being played here but also in the business that wraps around it being viable in the long term. That was the mission. It was never to make money for myself, as my critics at ECB might suggest. In fact, all I've done to date is put quite a lot of my own money into it.'

Professional sport has often been bankrolled by short-term cash injections into ailing clubs, but Bransgrove never saw the point in giving £10 million to cash-strapped Hampshire, only for the club to go under if he moved on. Unless some other benefactor came along, of course. His ambition has been to create something that becomes self-perpetuating, and not reliant only on cricket. Will it work? Check it out in *Wisden* in 20 years time. As things stand, the Rose Bowl is what building a dream is all about. A few hundred years ago entrepreneurial Englishmen went out and built an empire; these days they think that making money is sufficiently ambitious and its own achievement. Something like the Rose Bowl may be all that remains for modern-day English entrepreneurs and adventurers.

For all Rod Bransgrove's thoughts on committees, what is one man's aspiration in Hampshire is a committee's collective responsibility for Gloucestershire. They've had one-day internationals allocated, having bid successfully for a package of three going through to 2014. Indeed, they were the only Category B ground bidding. Now all they need is the TSF2-compliant venue in which to play them. Although they've been staging one-day internationals at the County Ground in Bristol since the 1999 World Cup, the TSF2 clock has been running down of late; if anything, their competitors for major matches may have stolen a march on them. Certainly by the time their redevelopment gained planning consent in 2010 there was no guarantee of games beyond 2014. Why so much ambition, then, when the long-term future for a 'field of dreams' is uncertain?

'We're not saying we have to run Test matches,' said chief executive Tom Richardson. 'Indeed we have been given a very clear steer that new entrants to the Test arena will not be allowed unless one of the present incumbents drops out. But we do want to continue running one-day internationals and T20 internationals. And we also want to improve our facilities for members and spectators, have better corporate hospitality, conferencing and banqueting facilities, and continue to grow the gymnasium membership. The much repeated maxim of needing to bring in income 365 days a year remains key.

'We obviously need more new facilities. We've already put in new changing rooms, ice baths and balconies because before that we had the players changing in one area and watching from another. That was useless. Internationally and domestically it's important they're together in one place.'

Paul Millman can testify to the standards that international teams expect these days. The Australians in particular were no-holds barred in their criticism of the facilities they found at Canterbury. Not that this stopped Steve Waugh spending five weeks at the St Lawrence ground at the back end of 2002. There must have been an Ashes series coming over the hill.

However, it was the carrot of international cricket rather than Aussie comforts that spurred Kent towards the restoration tragedy that befell them in the first decade of the new century. True, they were unlucky in their timing, in a way that Somerset, say, were not. For after the initial outlay of a million pounds in planning and legal fees, give or take, their aspirations were knocked off course by the financial problems being encountered by their enabling developer, Persimmon. In December 2008 Persimmon pulled out of a £7 million deal to build 72 houses, money that was earmarked to help finance the ground improvements. There was no joy for the county on their other major income project, either. Despite having planning permission for a 130-bed four-star hotel fronting the Old Dover Road, one vital ingredient was absent – a hotel partner willing to take on the development.

When an ill-conceived venture into pop-concert promotion backfired badly in 2009, there seemed no end to Kent's woes. Winning promotion in the Championship might have been consolation for their members – some of whom had bothered to vote in the proposed ground development plan – but it did nothing to improve the club's balance sheet. Ironically, when another builder eventually stepped in to rescue the housing enterprise, Kent were on their way back down to Division Two in the Championship.

It was as if the Furies had turned their back on the county for their hubris in bidding to be more than the domestic county club in which a rich cricketing heritage was rooted. This after all was the ground where grown men tugged their forelock at the mere mention of Lord Harris and bent a knee at the sight of M.C. Cowdrey or E.W. Swanton. On his first day as chief executive, Paul Millman had been phoned by the latter and told to be ready at midday to take him to lunch. It was as if Jimmy Porter had never been born. But biting into the apple of international cricket at the 1999 World Cup had led Kent into temptation and they had over-reached themselves. Their old ground needed better facilities, there's no denying that. But as Jim Swanton would have reminded them had he been alive, it needed to remain a cricket ground, not become a venue or, God forbid, a stadium.

Could Kent's difficulties be lying in wait for Gloucestershire? Or had they put together a business model that was strong enough to get them through the troughs of economic fluctuations? One thing was certain. They couldn't claim they'd been seduced by the ECB's dangled carrot. Anything but, Tom Richardson thought. 'If we turned round and said that we're not going to do it, I don't think anybody at Lord's is going to try to persuade us that we should. Having said that, they've been supportive in what we're doing.

'We have, however, had to look again at our plans and scale them down. We're now looking to raise the majority of the funding from our enabling development [to provide student accommodation] and will aim for a new media centre, improvements to the pavilion including hospitality and conferencing, improvements to the practice facilities and an increase in permanent seating to circa 8,000. Above all,' he emphasised, 'we're seeking to reduce our borrowing to a minimum.'

After some of the borrowings that counties have committed to, that strategy must be sweet music to Gloucestershire's membership, which is at the heart of the philosophy behind this project. Indeed, Richardson set out his stall on the premise that Gloucestershire are a county cricket club, a members club. 'We've been going since 1871, been on this ground since 1888, and we want to keep that going. We want to thrive in that form, but we've got to move with the times if we want to grow. If this all comes together, three things will continue to make us money. Obviously cricket, in other words gate income, corporate hospitality, sponsorship and advertising. Cheltenham [cricket] Week will continue to be a good influence on turnover as will Twenty20, and then there's conferencing and the gym. So the business of cricket we view as everything from winning on the field through to the academy producing cricketers, and then all the peripheral commercial things. But ultimately it's all about having a successful team and having the money on a permanent basis to be able to do that.'

The gym is interesting, for Gloucestershire have bucked the trend in making a success of their gym. Derek Brewer closed down the one at Trent Bridge. At Worcester they don't even run to an indoor school on site. They go to Malvern College, which in addition to indoor nets, can provide a gym, swimming pool, squash courts and more in its £12 million sports centre. Yet Gloucestershire's proposal to update their gym, and include a swimming pool, was a key feature of their planning application.

'We've built the gym up from nothing to raising between £300,000 and £400,000,' Richardson said. Its contribution to Gloucestershire's 2010 turnover was a healthy £307,000, which is possibly more than the other counties manage together from gym income. The pre-development facilities may not look pretty, but they're functional, effective and popular. Having the City of Bristol College on the door-step can't do any harm either. 'We've gone from having half a man and a dog working there to having it manned full time. We provide classes, courses, one-to-one training, it's a really good local amenity. The other thing is that we allow our gym members to be cricket members. Logistically they come into the ground anyway and so once in they're part of it.'

For those who like their cricket it's a great deal. And for the club it could be an enterprising way of getting others to take a more active interest in the game and Gloucestershire cricket. Beyond that, the gym maintains the club's link with the community, complementing their interaction with schools and social organisations in Bristol and the wider county. Tom Richardson had a ready example to hand, pointing across the ground to the former playing fields once used for car parking. There's a primary school there now.

'In future we'll have less of their land for parking, so we have had to adjust our development plan to create more parking spaces. However, as part of our growing relationship with the school, we're going to allow them to play football on our outfield. Now that is quite a nice thing to do. It's part of our ground being used in the community, and a bunch of school kids running up and down on it won't do us any harm. In fact we're actually taking the school under our wing so it will be like a junior academy of sorts. We're going to send players over there to help with some coaching, and others to help them with reading, and we'll try to get it the right way round,' he joked. 'We also allowed them to use our education centre for three to four months as a reception class when they weren't going to be ready to start school in September.'

Along with community interaction there is another value that the club can offer Bristol. Cricket is the only major sport providing international competition there. So even with Cardiff 40-odd miles away, there has to be a market for a 20,000-capacity international ground in a city of around 430,000, not forgetting the whole of the south-west with its motorway and rail links to Bristol. If there isn't, the problem isn't one for Gloucestershire's business model alone; it's one for English cricket as a whole. It would throw into contention its entitlement to be considered a major national game. As for Gloucestershire's plans, the alternative to not proceeding would be to downsize and maybe even up sticks. Sell off the Bristol site to developers and settle down in Gloucester, say, with a modern but less ambitious Category C county ground.

Such a move would not sit well with Bristol's city fathers, especially when taking into account the University of the West of England's economic impact study that supported Gloucestershire's planning application. A Test match, even if it doesn't come into the club's current thinking, would be worth something like £5 million to Bristol. A World Cup or World Twenty20 game would boost the economy by about £4.3 million. And of course there'd be the worldwide television audience to whom Bristol and the ground's state-of-the-art facilities would be showcased.

However, with Category A grounds at Southampton and Cardiff in approximate geographical competition with Bristol, there is a corridor of uncertainty running from the Rose Bowl to the Swalec Stadium. The Major Match Group will have their work cut out when they're marking those balanced scorecards, and for all Gloucestershire's aspirations there's the rub. At the risk of repetition, there just aren't enough major matches to go round. Had there been a capacity strategy for international cricket in England (and Wales), and had the ECB addressed the implications of that strategy, it is possible that much of the debt and uncertainty, the talk of franchises and counties going to the wall, could have been avoided.

Cardiff may indeed get along by being a conference business with a cricket ground attached – as chairman Paul Russell has reportedly said. And the Rose Bowl may one day be an international sports and entertainment complex in which cricket is a player but not necessarily the whole band. But it seems to me that cricket is the essence of Gloucestershire's business plan. The add-ons make a contribution, but the business plan expects a regular injection of major match income in order to be sustainable. It's a big roll of the dice.

Maybe having its own railway station would help the ground. It did wonders for the Arsenal once upon a time, even if admittedly that was a long time past. The romance of the railway linked to the romance of county cricket; both dear to English hearts, both centrally supported and both loss making. Imagine alighting from the train at Ashley Hill station as men, women and children did in the 19th century to see W.G. Grace play, even to watch him practising. The station, closed since 1964, would be ideal for travellers coming from either Temple Meads station in the city centre or Bristol Parkway on the outskirts. Gloucestershire's redevelopment plans already include an improved approach to the ground – another box ticked on the balanced scorecard – but having its own bespoke railway station would be a real vote-winner. With the City of Bristol College attracting more and more students into the area, government policies notwithstanding, it could even become a community asset. It's worth a thought.

CHAPTER NINE
MAKING A
DIFFERENCE

When Jim Cumbes was starting out as a professional cricketer at the beginning of the 1960s, he'd sometimes get into conversation with a neighbour from up the road. 'I used to see him at the weekend and he would talk my socks down on cricket, which was smashing for me as a young lad. He'd go on about Washbrook and Statham and so forth, all the Lancashire players, and I said to him one day, "How often do you get down to the ground?" "Jim," he said, "I'm ashamed to tell you, I've never been in my life." "How do you know so much about it?" I asked, and he said, "It's the first page I read in the morning."

'He knew the averages, he knew who was getting runs, who was in form, he even knew when I was getting wickets in the second team because in those days the papers had the second eleven scores abbreviated. He knew all that but he'd never been to a game at Old Trafford. I found it amazing.'

He's not so amazed any more. He still finds himself in conversation with people who are ever so knowledgeable about Lancashire, who's playing and who shouldn't be playing, what's gone wrong mid-season after they'd had such a good start. And he knows if he asked them the last time they'd seen Lancashire play, the answer would like as not be, not for a couple of years. The truth might as easily be, never.

Down at Edgbaston, Colin Povey had a different take on another variation of the same story. 'Historically there's been little accurate information about how many days of cricket and what types of game cricket fans actually come to. We can all compartmentalise the traditional county member as a lover of the four-day game who comes to every home match that Warwickshire ever play, and they go and watch the second team as well, doesn't matter what day of the week it is. Well, in reality that is not true.'

It hasn't been true for many years, though not everyone has wanted to accept it as fact. For too long myths and memories kept the game alive in conversations and in print, but you can't run businesses on the perceived influence of traditional members.

'Most members only come to a handful of games,' Northants chief executive Mark Tagg says. 'They want to come down to the ground, chat with their friends, have a cup of tea and enjoy *the game*. They don't care always who's batting or bowling; they enjoy *the game*. And in its purest sense, I suppose, that's support, isn't it?'

Too right it is and, as county treasurers would tell you, that kind of support is still a source of income to a club. It's just not sufficient, that's all, providing approximately nine per cent of the county game's annual turnover. However, we shouldn't underestimate the value of those members' long-term contributions. They might appear to be low-value subscribers in a season's accounts but most likely they will be subscribers for 10, 20, 30 years. And as well as being loyal supporters of the county game, a high proportion of them will also be England followers and purchasers of international tickets. County members may have a greater value than an individual year's subscription.

Sometimes it occurs to me that there's a touch of the Church of England about county cricket: a good turnout on high days, and occasionally on holidays, a small but faithful attendance for the weekly diet, not too much knowledge or undue concern about what's going on behind the scenes, solid opposition to any suggestion that the institution is no longer relevant or its days are numbered. There's a thesis there on the attitude of the English to their institutions, and I'm sure it's been written many times already. But the truth, I suspect, is that it's human nature as much as the nature of the English to support the things we value only when they're threatened. Too often we take our customs and our cultures for granted, which is why it is easy to drop in and drift out of them. The rituals of smells and bells, of bat and ball, are familiar and comforting. They reassure us that all the simple certainties are still here, despite the fact that we've been away so long. Or like Jim Cumbes's neighbour, never been at all but always a believer.

I've met many in England over the years intensely unhappy at what they perceive has been the loss of an England that once was – whatever it was and when. And I can sympathise with what they mean – with where they are coming from – because so often they are coming from somewhere they never went back to often enough. They always expected it to be there and one day it wasn't. That's why, by the end of my travels and my conversations, I'd overcome my long-held cynicism about the worth of county cricket and had replaced it with an appreciation of the relatively small group of men and women who are holding together their piece of the English mosaic.

When asked what motivated him and his colleagues around the country, Durham's David Harker replied, 'because it's cricket, because we still think that the sport matters. It's an important part of our culture. If you go to a football club or a rugby club and ask them why they do what they do, they want to be successful on the field. If you talk to people in cricket you don't necessarily get that as an answer. It may be, "We're trying to produce players for England," but I'm not sure how many of them actually are driven by the desire to win cricket matches. We have a very active Cricket Foundation that uses the game to try to benefit our local communities and that means something. We have the opportunity to make a difference to people's lives through the sport. Yes, you can do that in any sport, but cricket and the spirit of cricket stand for something. It gives us and the sport a particular place within our communities.'

Jim Cumbes would go along with that. As with Tom Richardson at Bristol, he found an opportunity for community involvement right on his Old Trafford doorstep. He wasn't so sure, however, that county cricket has always been socially aware of the need to accept some responsibility for its locality. A sense of place in the community was not always a consideration, let alone a prime concern.

'I feel sometimes that cricket clubs, certainly this one, have never been that involved in the local community. We were almost that club the other side of the brick wall. And I think cricket has suffered because of that. Even local councillors used to say, "Your game's an elite sport". Elite sport, I'd say, look at the old photos and all the cloth caps. How can you tell me that's elite? But they had a point.

'When we do the development to the ground,' he went on, 'we're specifically building the media centre so that the new academy school here can use it in the winter months as an IT centre, a business centre or whatever it is they want. That way we are linking in with the community, and it's a very poor community around here. A lot of unemployment, a lot of Asian kids at the school over there. So if we can say to them, you can have that as a classroom during the winter months, they'll snatch our hand off. They've done it already. We've also said, now we've got an outfield with new drainage, if you need a football pitch play out there. They're not going to damage it, 14-year-olds.'

The provision of community facilities has similarly been a plank in Surrey's ground development programme. 'You can be tremendously community friendly,' chief executive Paul Sheldon said, 'but what's that worth if you don't have facilities for the community to use when they come to the ground.' So when Surrey built their spectacular new OCS Stand at the Vauxhall end of The Oval, there were, in addition to the revenue-earning conference rooms and hospitality suites, several facilities for after-school activities, among them the nationwide Playing for Success scheme. Pride of place goes to the Ben Hollioake Learning Centre, named after the popular young England and Surrey all-rounder who lost his life in a car accident in 2002. Complete with computers and other learning aids, it provides study support for local schoolchildren in a safe, friendly environment.

'We have two people permanently working on community activities and community liaison,' Sheldon added. 'As well as the provision for education there are activities to get kids off the streets. We also liaise closely with the local residents to keep them properly informed about all the planning applications we have going through. That's a big investment, having two people who are there to improve our relations with the local community and make sure that we are part of Lambeth and the whole area, which it has to be said is a very needy one.'

Through such community activities, however, an affinity with the cricket club may develop, and that in turn could lead to much more in the multi-cultural society that England has become. Integration into an existing, tradition-seeped structure requires a lot more than one-way traffic. There has to be a welcoming hand, a warm embrace. A day at the Test match, cheering on India or Pakistan in the company of parents or mates, is a far remove culturally and socially for a teen-age Asian-English boy or girl who might wonder about going to a county ground for a domestic match, a Twenty20 say. The photos of those bygone cloth caps could even act as a barrier to belonging. But games of football on the county ground outfield might foster a sense of belonging; it can be their ground as well.

It's not going to happen tomorrow, it's going to take generations probably. Taking a taxi back to Leicester station after talking to David Smith, Paul and I got talking to the driver. More to the point he got talking to us on the assumption that, picked up at Grace Road, we must be interested in cricket. He loved talking about cricket, he told us. He was passionate about Sachin Tendulkar, had his own ideas who should be captaining Pakistan, was sure England would beat Australia when they went 'down there'. And on weekends, if he wasn't working, he played cricket for his local village. He loved cricket. Did he ever watch Leicestershire? Paul asked. No, he only watched inter-national cricket. On television.

'We're living in a city where 50 per cent of our population is Asian,' David Smith had told us earlier, 'and the club needs to reflect Leicester's multi-cultural nature. We're well represented in all the county age-group squads from 11 to 16 until they get to GCSEs.

Their parents tend to pull them out of sport then because they want them to focus on academics. Our challenge is to get the parents to understand that actually sport and academics can work together and that many of the skill bases that you learn in sport will assist you in academics. An Asian county cricketer going through into the England team could make a major difference, because like it or not that is where the focus is now. If Adil Rashid at Yorkshire, say, could win a permanent place for England, that would have a massive impact on Asians in pursuing a cricket career.'

You'd like to think so, but linking representation to ethnicity is not necessarily a straightforward matter. It can also concentrate the mind on the difference, as philosopher Julian Baggini pointed out in an essay on identity, 'If we think that we need people "like us" to represent us, we inevitably get a stronger sense of being different from those who are not like us.'

Nor will representation alone bring people from the ethnic communities into the grounds. As Notts' chief executive Derek Brewer knows, you can't expect people to come of their own volition, even to an international game. 'These are not easy markets to crack, so you've got to go out there and do it.'

Doing it led the club to teaming up with the local Karimia Institute and the Bobbersmill Mosque to promote cricket at Trent Bridge. They put up multi-lingual posters publicising forthcoming international matches and Brewer went on Nottingham's Asian network radio with a member of the institute. Notts made sure halal food was available for Muslim spectators and that there were prayer facilities inside the ground.

However, the club is no stranger to undertaking initiatives in local communities, and, Brewer admits, they have refocused their whole *raison d'être* over the past few years. 'I can recall when I was at RBS, working with a number of businesses and looking at the question, "What is a business for?" At face value this appears to be a very obvious question, but when you start asking whether it is for customers, stakeholders, shareholders or employees then it's actually quite a hard question to answer.

'Both as a senior management team here, and then with the general committee, we went through this process. As a result, back in 2006, we placed our community work and the aspiration of increasing participation in the game as core rather than peripheral objectives. We set up the Trent Bridge Community Sports Trust to ensure that our words were translated into actions, and reaffirmed our commitment to make a real difference to people in Nottinghamshire, be it through schools, inner city areas or recreational clubs. As ever the quality of people is central to success, and we appointed Tracey Francis from Sport England to head up this work.'

During the winter months, for example, the Trust runs its Trent Bridge Classroom project three days a week in the ground's press box. An initiative to reward schools that have gone the extra yard in incorporating cricket within their curriculum, it offers a day's experience at Trent Bridge for 30 to 36 eight- to ten-year-olds and their teachers. The club provides each child with a colourfully produced cricket-related workbook covering four subjects – geography, history, literacy and numeracy – and the day ends with an hour's cricket in the indoor nets. When Trent Bridge hosted the ICC World Twenty20 in 2009, the Trust took the initiative a step further and produced teacher resource booklets for every primary school in Nottinghamshire. The programme's motto is, 'Making learning fun through cricket'. Making cricket make a difference to its community is maybe a way of giving meaning to that recent political buzzword, localism. Or am I confusing localism with the big society? Never mind, it's a big issue whichever way you look at it.

For Brewer, further inspiration came in September 2007 when ICC hosted a worldwide gathering of chief executives to coincide with the first ICC World Twenty20. 'After the conference I spent four days in Cape Town watching some more matches in the tournament, and it was there that I saw an outstanding Positive Futures programme in action. Seeing the way in which Western Province Cricket Club and other sporting bodies had come together to inspire youngsters, I felt that such a programme could have a real impact in Nottingham. When I returned to Trent Bridge, Mark Worrall, our business development manager, and I worked together and we raised £200,000 from the Football Foundation as a contribution to a sustainable three-year project. Then when Tracey arrived in 2008, she made the whole thing happen, appointing people to key roles.'

The Positive Futures programme in the United Kingdom is built around a four-way partnership between the Home Office, Sport England, the Football Foundation and the Youth Justice Board. Its aim is to encourage young people at risk of social exclusion to take part in sports and leisure activities as a way to improve their quality of life, both currently and in the future. Research has shown the extent to which sport can provide skills and experience needed later in life, along with leading to improved health, better results at school, better job prospects and a reduction in offending.

'Obviously the level of deprivation in Nottingham is nothing near what it is in Cape Town,' Brewer continued, 'but there were opportunities for us to help here all the same. When we got our development loans from the local authorities, I'd said to each of the three chief executives, "What would you like us to do in return?" It was the first time they'd been asked that question. Allen Graham, a visionary CEO at Rushcliffe Borough Council, said, "We've got a problem with four streets in Cotgrave; we'd like you to work with the kids there." Cotgrave is a disadvantaged area of Nottinghamshire, so with £125,000 of funding from the Football Foundation we set up our Positive Futures programme there. We're one of the first cricket clubs to receive funding from the Football Foundation for a project, and it's been fantastic. From the club's point of view it's given us massive profile and it's really helped us with the local authorities.

'It's a three-year programme with a dedicated cohort of 25 youngsters which extends annually, and to date we have engaged more than 50 per cent of the total population of young people in the 10 to 19 age bracket. Our core programme delivers traditional sports and adventure activities, and each programme is created by the young people themselves.

'It runs throughout the year, but more importantly it's directed through service providers identifying young people at risk and it operates at times when juvenile crime peaks. Therefore school holidays, Friday nights and weekends are core delivery times. Initial statistics produced by Nottinghamshire Police have shown a huge correlation between our work and a reduction in juvenile crime. It's groundbreaking social exclusion work through cricket.'

The club's thinking outside the cricket box produced an unexpected financial spin-off for Trent Bridge as well. Their invitation to Olympic gold medallist Kelly Holmes to attend their England v Australia one-day international in 2009 resulted in the Dame Kelly Holmes Legacy Trust booking the ground's conference facilities, while for the Cotgrave kids there was a personal visit from Kelly herself.

'It was all over local television,' Brewer said, 'and these kids had never been on television before, so it was an amazing afternoon for them. What we've done there, it's been like a spider's web, spreading outwards. We're seen locally as being pioneers in that field.'

Another social exclusion project with which Nottinghamshire have become involved, the Say Yes campaign, uses Trent Bridge as a hub and entails working with partner agencies in Nottingham's inner-city areas. It's a 12-week programme for 50 youngsters from the hardest areas, working in groups with business people acting as mentors. Trent Bridge staff are among the business mentors.

'The first one of these,' Brewer said, 'I'll never forget it. We had the launch at Trent Bridge, 50 kids and they were absolutely running amok, going all over the place. They'd never been in a cricket ground before. The thing is, we'd messed up the date and there was a County Championship match going on at the same time. I got this call over the PA to see a group of very angry members. So off I went to talk to them, and asked what the problem was. "These kids," they said, "what are they doing here, running around? This is a Championship game," etc, etc. I looked them all in the eye and said very slowly, "If you knew the problems these kids have, you would support what we're doing in its entirety." I didn't have to explain anything further.

'So the kids are running amok in week one. By week 12 we have an end-of-programme event with 200 people in the audience. The groups had each been working on anti-social behaviour programmes and had to do a presentation on them at the event. I was on the judging panel. That afternoon, I walked around the ground and there were all these kids in their different groups, concentrating on preparing the PowerPoint presentations they were making that evening to their parents and peers. It was fantastic, unbelievable. The parents were in tears, I almost had tears in my eyes myself when I did the closing speech. It was so fantastic seeing this untapped potential being realised.'

Not all counties have managed Nottinghamshire's level of community commitment but, generally speaking, outreach has a role in what they all do. Some 20 miles west along the A52, Derbyshire chief executive Keith Loring, one time chief exec of Derby County Football Club, has been getting kids off the street by staging community events at his ground's Gateway Centre, a joint enterprise involving the regional development agency, Sport England and the county club. Like Brewer, he has made working with the local community a priority since taking over the chief executive role in October 2008. His background in football introduced him to community work, and one of his former clubs, Brentford, won a national award during his time at Griffin Park. In his few years in charge at Derbyshire, Loring has re-introduced the community gymnasium as well as dance classes and martial arts. A boxing tournament was staged in 2010 on behalf of a local boxing club.

'Of course we make sure we do everything we can to increase the cricket coaching facilities here at the club,' he said. 'Every child under 12 in Derbyshire is entitled to free membership of Derbyshire County Cricket Club, regardless of whether they attend cricket courses or not. However, the courses can be a helpful vehicle from which to engage them.'

As he himself would probably say, Keith Loring gets up early in the morning. Get the kids onside and the kids will bring parents. He knows he has a haul on his hands to turn Derbyshire around after some grim years, but he has been doing it without running up debts and by investing in the club's facilities to gain more interest in the county and to attract and develop local young cricketers, both boys and girls.

'We get very good feedback from our members, they're proud of the fact that the club has come to where it is from where it was. Now we're instilling a lot of pride back into this club. The most important thing we need to do now is assist the head of cricket, John Morris, in strengthening the team. That's why everything we're doing to the ground we're doing within our resources so that any extra money earned goes straight into cricket.'

No wonder he was narked when Mark Nicholas said that Derbyshire were one of the first-class counties that exist without any obviously justifiable reason. Oh well, to give C. L. R. James another run for his money, what do they know of cricket who only cricket know? At the time I met Loring, Derbyshire were involved in a major coaching programme for schoolchildren, they'd announced a profit for the fourth year in a row, they had some promising young cricketers coming through. There are worse things in life than being picked on by a highlights front man.

Much of the recent investment in the grass roots has, of course, been due to the ECB putting more money than ever into recreational cricket. This can be traced back to England winning the Ashes in 2005, but the planning that preceded it dates back to the establishment of the ECB itself, and to the appointment of Ian MacLaurin as its first chairman. Being one of the country's most successful retailers, he appreciated how important advertising and marketing were in product promotion, so it was understandable that early on he was talking of the England team as cricket's shop window. Get a successful England team and the benefits would flow down from that, was his message. It came to define his chairmanship of the ECB: the grass roots can't flourish without the financing that comes in at the top end of cricket, and equally a successful England team isn't possible without participation and identification of talent at the grass roots. Achieving that, as Tim Lamb explained, required a top-to-bottom reform of the way English cricket was structured.

'In the same way that we took initiatives to improve the quality of the England team, which ultimately led to more focused coaching, greater rewards for the players and central contracts, equally we completely restructured the development side. Once the National Cricket Association had amalgamated with the ECB, we created a new development department under Keith Pont, who takes a lot of the credit for putting in place a very effective development structure. That meant the right level of financing for the grass roots, for coaching facilities, helped initially by more Community Lottery Sports Fund money than is available now. But that was the model, recognising the interdependence between the grass roots and the elite; that one can't survive without the other. Perhaps it took longer than we would have liked to transform the England team into a winning team, because it was nine years following the formation of the ECB before England actually won the Ashes. The rest though is history, and it certainly was a great boost.'

One outcome of the restructuring that Tim Lamb mentioned was the creation of 39 County Cricket Boards (CCBs) to be investment and development vehicles for recreational cricket, independent of the first-class counties. 'The cricket boards do a great job around the country,' Jim Cumbes said. 'We've got the Lancashire Cricket Board here at Old Trafford, and Andy Hayhurst and his crew do a fantastic job. I think they've got the highest number of focus clubs, bigger than Yorkshire. A lot of schools are involved with local cricket clubs now, and there's something like 70,000 kids playing cricket in the north-west.'

Coming under the aegis of the Recreational Assembly, the CCBs provide a ring-fenced pathway for government funding, while at the same time allaying fears that too much ECB money ends up in the hands of the first-class counties – or more to the point in the salaries of professional cricketers. But while the separation of professional and recreational cricket was a rationale for the existence of a county board – Derbyshire CCB, say, in the same county as a first-class club, Derbyshire CCC – the logic seems less applicable to having a CCB and a Minor County Cricket Association (MCCA) in the same county. It has led to some pretty substantial bureaucratic beasts roaming around the recreational hinterland and to hear Dave Brooks tell it, there's a substantial bureaucracy feeding them.

'Our county board head of cricket, who looks after Sussex recreational cricket, has six ECB contacts for different things: one for recreational management, one for facilities, one for volunteers, etc. It's as if almost every initiative that comes along ends up creating five jobs. One is the national leader and then four regional leaders, and it ends up with us having six contacts. All the other boards clearly have six contacts, and that becomes much harder for the minor counties because they haven't got all the in-house officers to deal with it. With them it's often all volunteer work. There must be more efficient ways for it to be managed.'

Middlesex chief executive Vinny Codrington is just as critical of the bureaucracy that has grown up around the recreational game. 'Years ago we ceded more power to the ECB in the hope that they'd provide leadership and they're not. They're providing management; they provide more and more management, and this means there are more and more of them. So my worry is a fundamental one. We've got too much bureaucracy within the recreational game, and in part that's because some of it is government led with money coming from

Sport England or whoever. If I'm Old Actonians or Ealing, say, what I want is help in the areas where I need help, which basically means money. It could be for nets, a new roller, a groundsman or better facilities, and for that they don't want some bureaucracy interfering. Instead we've got more and more big brother coming down on the local clubs and I worry for them.'

There's certainly an impression around the counties that the recreational gravy train has picked up speed over the last ten years. More people who used to volunteer their time to coach on a few evenings a week are now being paid, thanks to the funding coming into the game.

'The amount of money available to fund community coaches has driven the participation increases since 2005,' Dave Brooks said. 'Yes, we had the momentum from the Ashes, but it was the coaches out in the clubs who delivered the increases, and since then a lot of the community coaches have made a career out of coaching. Some are employed only part-time by their county boards, but that creates maybe 20 hours of work that pays the bills, if you like, and then they can add on schools, clubs and one-to-one coaching, that kind of thing.'

In the decade and a half since the CCBs were established, several of the first-class counties have more or less begun bringing the boards within the compass of their own operation. Governance and accounts are kept separate, but in most other respects the CCC and the CCB might just as well be one. The perception at Essex is such that you'd never know the two weren't integrated, David East said. 'I'm chief executive of both, and we have a joint brand called Essex Cricket that embraces both the county cricket club and the county board. You ask anyone among the players and staff who they work for and they would say Essex Cricket. The only reason we separate the county board and county club is for operational responsibility, for accountability.'

Meanwhile at Northamptonshire the cricket board has become a wholly owned subsidiary of the county club. 'The board and us are as one,' is how Mark Tagg described their position. 'We have to be so that everyone within the county's cricket community knows what we at Northants Cricket are trying to do.'

Naturally, this being England and English cricket, it's not the same situation everywhere. There are parts of the country, the north being an example, where the county clubs and county boards are not as integrated. That may come down to strong local leagues jealously protecting their traditions and territories, while with cross-county leagues no one county board is really responsible. As for some of the leagues in Yorkshire and Lancashire, the story goes it can be open warfare – not between the county board and the leagues, but between the leagues themselves. They're all so fiercely independent; they're a law unto themselves. And always have been.

David Smith was one of those with reservations about the first-class clubs embracing the county boards, certainly to the extent that Essex and Northamptonshire have. 'I see that as a conflict of interest personally. I think the board needs to be separate; the finances need to be separate. It is a difficult one, because the recreational game is clearly important, and all the county age-group squads come through the recreational game in effect. Therefore your cricketers of the future are in the hands of the boards, and some people can be a bit uncomfortable about that. Generally I think the county boards and the county cricket clubs should have a good working relationship, but finances should be separate.'

Given the sums of money flowing out of the ECB's central coffers into the recreational game, Smith makes a sensible point, especially as one or two first-class counties reckon the distribution that supports recreational cricket has grown out of proportion to their own cash-strapped needs. In 2008, recreational funding was £16.4 million, almost 17 per cent of ECB turnover, with close on £5.5 million going to the county boards. The following year it jumped by 30 per cent to £21.3 million, though the distribution to the county boards dipped to £4.8 million.

'To be fair to the ECB,' Dave Brooks said, 'they can claim credit for attracting Sport England money. By the sport applying for one significant grant, I suspect we get more than the 39 counties would if we were all applying individually.'

Sport England's four-year grant of £37.8 million up to 2013, for example, helped to boost the Cricket Foundation's 'Chance to Shine' programme, which since 2005 has been getting cricket back into state schools and directing youngsters towards local clubs. But projected government cutbacks and uncertainty over the level of Sport England funding have left the first-class counties wondering who could end up bearing the costs of the county boards. Jim Cumbes was one of several chief executives to express concern that the ECB might try to shift responsibility for the recreational game to the county clubs.

'You get grants to run things, you employ people, you set up programmes and then suddenly the grants dry up. You start having to pay for things yourself. If that happens with the boards, it will hit the counties very hard.'

What troubled Dave Brooks as much was the impact that changes to the funding for coaches could have on the development game. Prior to 2009, the county boards had received some £2.3 million from Sport England's Club and Coach Fund, via its nine Regional Sports Boards. When that source dried up, the ECB's intention was to maintain a similar level of club and coaching funding, but their formula for distributing it meant that certain CCBs would receive less than they had under the previous arrangement. It was all to do with the way Sport England's Regional Sports Boards had distributed their largesse in the first place: something to do with the money having to be spent in the region that allocated it. Some regions got more, some less. The ECB intended to level that particular bureaucratic playing field, which meant some county boards would get less than they had previously and some would get more.

'There have been 33,000 coaches created in the last five years through the Sky Sports/ECB programme,' Brooks said, 'and while most of them do it for love of the game, the better ones have been able to devote enough of their time to it because there's been money available. It's important for there to be a number of people who can devote their lives to coaching, because in our area programmes and county age-groups you need decent coaches. If you have poor quality coaches at 8, 9, 10, 11, by the time the kids hit the good coaches at 13 they've missed out really. But if reduced funding levels mean that coaches have to become wholly freelance, rather than part-time contracted to the boards, I fear a lot of them would have to walk away.'

That's a sorry prognosis for what, in conjunction with the increasing participation in schools and clubs, has been an ECB success story. That success, however, has been built on a business plan which, if not always as precarious as some would have us believe, is nevertheless a shade unhealthy when much of the ECB's turnover has been derived from two streams: television rights and counties bidding for international matches. Should both sources come under pressure in the years ahead, the first-class clubs and the recreational game's bodies could find themselves sharing responsibility for cricket in their overlapping communities by dint of necessity as much as by choice.

CHAPTER TEN
IT'S OUR MONEY!

When heads of organisations resort to meaningless phraseology, it's time to head for the hills. Around the turn of the century, Tim Lamb began talking up the first-class counties as 'centres of excellence'. Excellent at what was never apparent, especially as the end product of these so-called centres, the England cricket team, usually fell some way short of what the pundits and the punters regarded as excellent. Even the ECB came round to this conclusion in time. They took the England players out of county cricket, put them under contract to the Board, employed specialists (often foreign) to coach them and, praise be, the charabanc became a greyhound. Where that left the counties was another matter. Not so much centres of excellence as development centres, maybe. Academies or even nurseries, perhaps. Tim Lamb quit calling them centres of excellence and instead started calling them businesses. Which is more or less where we have been all along.

So knock me over with a Gray-Nicolls if I didn't come across centres of excellence again in the ECB's annual report for 2009. Making reference to that year's £35.4 million fee payments to the first-class counties, finance director Brian Havill commented that these were paid 'in recognition of the costs they incur in participation in the Board's competitions'. The counties, he went on to say, 'are effectively 18 Centres of Excellence and the fees paid to them underpin the Board's objective of ensuring a vibrant domestic game in which our most talented players are prepared for international cricket through a structured and competitive first class programme.'

We could do with a woof or two here to determine which is the dog and which is the tail. Instead, let's look first at what's being said.

Cricket fogeys like me, and there are still some of us about, tend to think of first-class (note the hyphen) cricket as being matches scheduled for three or more days' duration. Call me old-fashioned, but I have a sorry feeling that Mr Havill's 'structured and competitive first class [no hyphen] programme' relates to anything from Twenty20 to the County Championship, as played by the first-class counties. Competitive it may try to be; structured, as many I spoke to made clear, it is not.

David East (Essex): 'There's a major bleating going on about the amount of cricket that's being played. We're trying to shoehorn so much into a season.'

Paul Sheldon (Surrey): 'We have this very, very incohesive fixture schedule which is too congested; is never fully agreed by all the counties; but it satisfies the commercial demands of sponsorship and broadcasting.'

David Harker (Durham): 'As a game we just don't seem always to get it from a spectator's point of view. We rarely put ourselves in the shoes of the spectator. How do we make this game easier, more accessible?'

Colin Povey (Warwickshire): 'In my short time in cricket, the immortal words "Domestic Structure Review" must have been mentioned more than any others.'

Vinny Codrington (Middlesex): 'Everyone agrees that we play too much cricket and nobody agrees too much of what.'

Matthew Fleming (MCC): 'Cricket is changing so rapidly that the products the county structure is designed to sell are no longer in kilter with the existing structure and with demand. It's time there was a proper, grown-up strategic review about cricket and the next 25 years.'

As for being paid to play in the Board's competitions, Vinny Codrington expressed with a fair degree of anger and frustration what most chief executives thought about that. 'Until we reverse the cycle of who runs the game, it's going to get crazier and crazier. We play three different kinds of cricket, and now they're telling us we have to play this number of under-22s and so many under-26s, just to get our money. It's our money. It's absolutely daft. And they want us to produce England players when I can only produce a second eleven quality of game because either they've taken the best players out of the game [on to ECB central contracts] or they're keeping overseas players out of the game, or they're telling me to play kids.'

Jim Cumbes was equally convinced that the county game was poorer from the unavailability of England players, whether for the senior side, the Lions or even age-group teams. 'People used to come here to Old Trafford to watch Lancashire play and they understood there were five Test matches when Brian Statham wouldn't be here, and Geoff Pullar wouldn't be here, but the rest of the time they were here and people came and they looked forward to seeing the England players. I know England players have to be rested, and I understand the international calendar, but I'm not utterly convinced about it. I still think there's more room for England players to play domestic cricket. They talked about a Twenty20 competition with England players. Well, they're not playing in it much of the time.'

It's something to think about next time you hear some ECB suit wittering on about the integrity of county cricket. If week in, week out the counties can't play their strongest teams, doesn't that threaten the integrity and value of the county game? Or is it that one man's integrity is simply another man's platitude? Not that David Smith deals in platitudes. He tells it how it is, straight down the line, which from memory was how he batted. 'We have an obligation to protect the integrity of our game,' he said, 'both from a Championship point of view and to make certain we have a game that's robust to hand down to the next generation. We have to be very careful that, while we want to expand the game, money can't become our god, and I believe it has to a degree.'

He wouldn't be alone in thinking that. Rod Bransgrove for one reckoned that the greed of the authorities had cost the counties

CRICKET-RELATED INCOME IN 2009

	Turnover	ECB Fee	Members (No.)	Gate Receipts
	£	£	£	£
Derbyshire[4]	2,181,761	1,612,375	137,201 (2,099)	164,801
Durham[1]	6,935,652	1,882,651	291,050 (4,135)	2,941,460
Essex[4]	4,399,516	1,666,802	423,483 (5,381)	908,668
Glamorgan[4]	11,595,374	2,286,318	557,222 (3,000)	5,997,635
Gloucestershire[1]	3,817,000	1,611,000	493,000 (3,648)	836,000
Hampshire[2]	4,500,000	1,982,000	593,000 (6,167)	649,000
Kent[2]	5,029,939	1,883,813	396,070 (3,849)	676,096
Lancashire[4]	12,214,104	1,995,883	528,637 (8,047)	1,985,438
Leicestershire[1]	2,506,024	1,744,923	92,568 (2,416)	112,619
Middlesex[4]	4,316,000	1,850,000	744,000 (8,612)	678,000
Northamptonshire[1]	2,892,131	1,692,584	115,559 (2,511)	299,975
Nottinghamshire[1]	7,179,906	2,216,000	463,000 (7,500)	1,156,000
Somerset[1]	4,500,624	1,735,058	502,101 (4,631)	517,360
Surrey[3]	25,465,000	1,679,000	1,324,000 (9,702)	5,456,000
Sussex[2]	5,873,068	2,194,845	374,932 (3,759)	1,094,363
Warwickshire[1]	15,685,067	1,748,179	425,000 (5,967)	7,022,522
Worcestershire[1]	3,035,846	1,939,088	422,292 (3,765)	346,563
Yorkshire[4]	8,449,219	1,666,935	744,579 (8,588)	3,841,369

[1] Year ending 30.9.2009   [2] Year ending 31.10.2009
[3] Year ending 30.11.2009   [4] Year ending 31.12.2009

NOTE: The above figures are an assessment extracted mostly from county Report and Accounts. The variation in accounting methods means that it is not possible to produce like-for-like figures. Some counties, for example, include prize money and competition payments in their ECB figure while others do not, and some include commercial activities within their cricket income.

their unique asset when it came to Twenty20 cricket. And he had a point for, as Tim Lamb remembered, the original purpose of the new format had been to give the counties a boost, not the ECB. 'The model was that the counties would retain their home gate income. It was a way of helping them be more self-sufficient financially. So although Twenty20 was a central initiative, we agreed that we wouldn't take the gate money in the way we took the gate money [at the time] from international games and major domestic cup matches. At a very early stage we made it clear to the counties that we were not looking for a part of the action.'

'The first year,' said Bransgrove, 'we were under instructions to play our top players. You make sure you pick X and Y, we don't want the format being devalued, they said. Hardly a year goes by and what happens? The ECB decide, "We'll play this as England," and the England players are taken out of our domestic Twenty20. The competition was immediately devalued and its *raison d'être* critically diluted.'

Just as questionable as the structure and the competitiveness of the playing programme, however, is the tune that underscores Brian Havill's passage. What it seems to be saying, in fact what it is saying, is that we, the ECB, pay this money to our centres of excellence, the 18 counties, because they do a job for us. They're behaving like the dog, whereas the counties regard them as the tail. 'It's our money,' Vinny Codrington said, and any one of the county chief executives could have uttered the same words. Quite a few did, and in doing so they brought into focus the conflict at the heart of the cricket business in England and Wales. What is the role of the counties? What is the role of the ECB? And whose money is it?

Neil Davidson has no qualms when it comes to giving a reasoned, businesslike point of view. As far as he is concerned, the first-class counties are 18 separate organisations who are members of a co-operative that provides income for them. When I suggested that English cricket looked more as if it were structured on a franchise model, with the ECB as the franchise holder, he was having none of it. People within the ECB might like it to be that way, he replied, and sometimes behave as if it is that way, but that's not how the ECB constitution works.

David East felt just as strongly. 'What we've got is 18 autonomous businesses working within a collective framework with central policies in terms of fixtures and the generation of income from international matches, sponsorship and TV rights. Those things are ceded to the ECB to collectively bargain for us. But we're not wholly owned subsidiaries of the ECB, we're independent businesses in the same way that there are 20 Premiership football clubs that are in exactly the same position. They use the Premiership framework to administer it and coordinate certain functions. Ultimately, we are all independent businesses and we all need each other in order to survive.'

And when it comes to the money? Davidson was adamant about the counties' entitlement to everything they received. 'I don't come from an apologist's point of view that we're dependent on handouts from the ECB; that without them we wouldn't be able to stand on our own two feet. That's not how it's set up. The counties are the owners of a business and that business is the ECB. Where I get out of my pram is on the way we're moving further and further away from the people who actually own the business. There's a popular view in the media that the first-class counties are too influential in English cricket. Well, I think the counties aren't influential enough.

'My analysis is this. The ECB is the governing body of the sport, but that's only one of its roles. If you look at the constitution, they're a cooperative more than anything else, with a common income that is split among the individual businesses. We in cricket have a common income, which is the revenue generated by international cricket basically. And that's the common income that gets spread among the counties, among the owners. So to say that no county is viable on its own is simply wrong, because we're all owners of the ECB, we're all owners of part of that international revenue. It's our money.'

With analyses like that, there must have been a few dry eyes at Lord's when Davidson stepped down as chairman of Leicestershire in October 2010 and so ceased being a member of the ECB. But while all the counties would agree with him that, 'It's our money', not all are in accord with the way the ECB distribute it these days. Some would sooner revert to the old days when the pot was basically divided by 17 and later 18 and they were left to spend it how they liked. As often as not on players who weren't eligible for England, which is one reason why in 2006 the ECB adopted a bipartite payment consisting of a fixed fee (FFP), paid in monthly instalments, and a performance-related fee (PRFP), based on county data from the previous year.

PRFPs were a major plank in the ECB's 2005 blueprint for cricket, *Building Partnerships – from Playground to Test Arena.* Its aims were to provide efficient leadership and governance, build a vibrant domestic game, encourage participation and following, particularly among the young, and develop successful England teams. Well, to almost quote Meatloaf one more time, two out of four ain't bad.

To help achieve those aims, the ECB set out five criteria as financial incentives to the counties, and these formed the basis of the initial PRFPs: England-qualified players; players selected for England at every level; the accreditation level of coaches in the county; the performance of ECB-accredited academies which develop young players to county level; and the delivery of sponsors' and media requirements. Since then the criteria have been extended to include playing England-qualified cricketers under 22 and under 26, as mentioned earlier by Vinny Codrington; providing crowd order management; improving field-of-play drainage and installing floodlights. For 2011 there was also a one-off payment for counties whose grounds were compliant with our old friend, TSF2 – as much as £250,000, some counties were hoping. It helps explain those development plans.

The non-Test match grounds, not so surprisingly, generally supported the performance-related payments because their business plans gave more weight to player development than to major capital-expenditure ground developments. 'Rewarding counties for improving and bettering themselves, and bettering the health of English cricket have been good measures,' said David East. 'Those aims are something we've worked towards and our infrastructure has delivered them. We've never been rewarded for it before, so now we're getting a reward for something we've always done.'

Not that the performance-related payments aren't without their idiosyncrasies. The money that the clubs are paid extra for playing under-22s, not so much extra for under-26s and even less extra for over-26s, all comes out of an agreed amount in the Memorandum of Understanding. What's left over after the distribution, it seems, is then divided up amongst the 18 counties, 'so after going through the whole exercise we all still end up getting the figure they first thought of,' said one bemused county treasurer. Emperor's new clothes, anyone?

Mark Tagg sounded as if he'd be happy for the PRFPs to go even further. 'I would be comfortable in concept with more weight going on PRFPs in terms of English-qualified players and preparing players for England, rather than having the basic distribution. Almost have no fixed fee at all, but just all about developing players. That would sharpen counties' focus.'

Not that all the counties would agree. 'I suppose 45 per cent of our income is through the ECB,' Tom Richardson said, 'and of that roughly 30 per cent is from the fixed fee and 15 per cent is performance related. It has been argued that we should be getting more in a straight fee payment, bearing in mind what we used to get. I think they're putting a lot of emphasis on whether you have England players, but you can't plan your business on people being selected for England. It becomes a precarious approach.'

There's more to it than selection for England, of course. Performance-related fees also relate to the number of games England-qualified cricketers play in pre-determined county competitions, which for their counties boils down to no play, no pay. A player out with injury or loss of form costs his county money, and you can't cost in contingencies like that when you're putting an annual budget together. As Tom Richardson implied, it's a precarious enough business without having to deal with unknowns.

Richardson has cut to the chase when it comes to the level of distribution that the counties receive. There's a feeling out there, particularly among the larger grounds, that the percentage of overall ECB turnover going to the stakeholders – the first-class counties, the minor counties, the cricket boards – has actually reduced. While the money distributed has increased, so the money being spent on such things as Team England, the National Academy at Loughborough and the infrastructure of the ECB itself has grown exponentially. In relative terms, the argument goes, the counties are worse off than they were a decade ago. Added to this, one concerned county boss told me, they have had to cope with the emergence of players' agents, who have had a dramatic effect on the wage bills. There is also increased pressure on wages from the relatively large sums earned now by England players, and this is highlighted when these players return to county cricket and expect comparative earnings. Whether the recent introduction of a county salary cap will stabilise the wage spiral remains to be seen because the cap has little relevance for many counties. Their wage bills do not approach it, but this does not mean they aren't under pressure to increase their salaries. People always want more if they can get it.

There is more to the performance-related fee payments than rewarding counties for bringing on young English cricketers, however. They have also made counties think twice about playing non-England-qualified players, and in particular those overseas hybrids known as Kolpaks. If they happen to sound like something out of *Dr Who*, that's because, with a little right-field thinking, you might say they're an alien device – all right then, a European Union ruling – to undermine the well-being of England's national interest. In cricket's case, that's beating Australia every two years. Or you could say that they're immigrant workers, welcomed into the shires because they're cheaper than

English players. As *Wisden* reported one county chief executive saying at the time the Yorkshire fast bowler, Steve Kirby, was up for grabs, 'We can buy three Kolpaks for one Kirby.'

Some would also claim that they provide better value as cricketers. Jim Cumbes agreed that PRFPs had been influential in getting some of the lesser-quality Kolpaks out of the county game, but he questioned the premise that there were too many non-England-qualified county cricketers. 'We had a lad here, Faf du Plessis, 25 years old, South African, prepared to live here and probably qualify for England. As they all do,' he chuckled. 'As a mentor for young cricketers he was fantastic. His attitude to the game through his lifestyle, his way with people, you couldn't fault the lad. He was a great example for our young cricketers to follow, and we lost him because he couldn't get a work permit. He used to take coaching sessions – our fielding improved beyond all recognition in Twenty20 and that was down to him. He set the standards and this would rub off on the English players.'

Cumbes compared the role the Kolpaks could fulfil with the example that overseas players set when they first became integral to county cricket in the 1960s. 'The fact that Lancashire were so successful in one-day cricket in the 1970s was down to the influence Clive Lloyd and Farokh Engineer had. But we're losing that now, that dedicated interest, if you like, in the county game.'

Cumbes will tell you that he played in a golden era. There wasn't a lot of money in the game but it provided a wonderful lifestyle. It afforded opportunities to travel abroad to play cricket, and it was also a time when players socialised together after the game. David Smith agrees with him, and although former players generally drift towards nostalgia when recalling their playing days, he like Jim Cumbes has had the advantage of lengthy stints in cricket on both sides of the boundary.

'The generation now are far better paid than we were,' he says. 'That's progress and I'm delighted with that. But they don't socialise with each other. They are very different from the generation I played with. They don't talk cricket necessarily, whereas I remember as a young cricketer standing in a corner at Colchester talking to Dennis Amiss and Mike Denness, and they were chatting about cricket and batting and for me it was part of a massive learning curve. Yes, it has moved forward, and we have to identify the positives, but we should also remember the importance of generations of cricketers passing the game down to younger players, teaching the game, and also what you can and can't do. My worry is that the more money that comes into the game, the less people pass on knowledge. They become more protective. There's more of the attitude that I'm not going to help you because you might end up stuffing me. That's a sad reflection on society, not just on cricket, because it's this massive win-at-all-costs scenario now.

'It's probably an old-fashioned thing to say, but in a two-horse race someone has to lose. You don't have to like it, but you have to respect the fact that you've been in a competitive situation and someone has to lose. We talk a lot about learning to win, and that's massively important, but we also have to learn to lose. We have to learn to pull out the positives from a loss and move forward, and I think that's something the game and society have almost lost. We no longer accept the fact that there has to be a loser; as long as it's them and not us, that's OK. It doesn't work that way and so we must be careful that we protect our game and all the positive elements in it.'

It wasn't so long ago, 2008 actually, that Smith's former county, Leicestershire, had as many as six South Africans on their books. Smith defends that decision, though admits that the club did lose members because of it. Six is a lot, but with 18 counties available to choose from, just how many England-qualified cricketers do the selectors need? There's a tendency in bureaucracies to measure progress by quantity rather than quality: governments set targets to cut hospital waiting lists or increase the number of children reading and writing by a certain age. True progress, the way I figure it, would lie with improved treatment, or reading and writing better things; better England-qualified cricketers playing county cricket, rather than merely more of them. If all the PRFPs are doing is keeping some not very good

English cricketers in employment, they're not really serving the needs of the England team. Now that centrally contracted England players so rarely feature in county cricket, and overseas cricketers are being kept to a minimum, there is a risk of the developing players going through the motions instead of having the opportunity to test their talent against experienced overseas cricketers of high-calibre ability.

When I came back in 2000 for a second stint as editor of *Wisden*, the England team contained three players who had learnt their cricket abroad – Andrew Caddick, Graeme Hick and Craig White – while the coach, Duncan Fletcher, hailed from Zimbabwe originally. Ten years down the line, with two divisions, central contracts and big Sky money, what do we find? England still dependent on players developed elsewhere, and the number could be more than three when they play Twenty20 internationals. As for the coach, while not the same one he nonetheless hailed from Zimbabwe and similarly knew how to beat Australia. There had been an interim English coach but he got the heave-ho after a contretemps involving a South African England captain, likewise heaved.

Still, as the Romans might have said – that inveterate scribbler, Edward Gibbon, could have said it for them – why go to all the bother of an empire if the children of the empire don't ultimately come and do the jobs your native citizens aren't up to? Matthew Fleming probably put his finger on it when he remarked in passing that Australia and South Africa have a better sporting and cricketing culture at all levels of their education. 'Their cream is of a higher quality than ours.' Oh well, or should that be, Oh wail! Let's give PRFPs ten years more and we'll see how much has changed as a result of the planned development initiatives. Assuming, of course, that the ECB and the counties are still in the same business.

CHAPTER ELEVEN
SACKS OF POTATOES

'English cricket is at something of a crossroads,' Matthew Fleming said thoughtfully, pausing while he picked the appropriate words to get his message across without sounding unduly alarmist. He'd already told me that this book would be overtaken by events before it was published, which was alarming enough. And when Lancashire and Yorkshire subsequently revealed losses of £2 million each in 2010 just as the manuscript went to the publisher, it looked as if he might be correct in his prediction. The game was truly in a pickle – not my word but an accountant friend's who, after looking through the counties' Reports and Accounts for 2009, reckoned half of them would be struggling to meet their interest payments in 2010 if their incomes showed no significant improvement. Not that the counties themselves had been hiding the fact that many of them were on week-to-week survival rations. If Mark Newton at Worcester was to be believed, 'the financial aspect of the game' wouldn't even be affected if three or four counties were to disappear. 'It'll scratch the surface,' he said.

So to temper the pessimism there was almost a note of optimism in Derek Brewer's resigned forecast that, 'in 12 months we will have limped along, which is the way it has always been.' And why not? Bumbling along is a national characteristic as well as a commentary on Sky television; has been for some time, I suspect. The 'amateurist attitude' of the English drove American philosopher William James to distraction when he visited Britain some 125 years ago, and doubtless it would today. Colin Povey at Edgbaston bemoaned the fact that 'for a professional sport cricket had remained incredibly, perhaps quaintly amateurish until very recently'. And yet, James was forced to concede, out of 'the blanket of apparent dullness and stupidity' can come 'the sanest, safest, deepest bits of insight'. No slouch when it came to psychology and religion, James called this 'a fascinating miracle' and I'd go along with that.

Matthew Fleming, however, was putting his money on common sense rather than miracles, being a tad more pragmatic when it came to cricket matters. 'Jazzer' had, after all, been a soldier as well as a county cricketer. 'The system as it is,' he said, 'certainly has conflicts and might not be robust enough to cope with the current evolution of cricket and the changing economic times. There's a real risk that part of the structure will break under the pressure. The challenge for us is to ensure that the constituent parts are mature enough to appreciate the breadth and depth of the evolution and to manage the change from within for the benefits of all, rather than allow self-interest to lead to a collapse and rebuild. I have no doubt that some of the more self-serving constituent parts have considered breaking away, but I'm hopeful that common sense will prevail.'

Fleming's hope chimes in with something South Korean economist Ha-Joon Chang wrote in his 2010 book, *23 Things They Don't Tell You about Capitalism*. 'The collective ability to build and manage effective organisations and institutions is now far more important than the drives and even the talents of a nation's individual members in determining its prosperity.' But when it comes to collectivism, because that's where we're coming to eventually, a much earlier economist possibly got closer to the root of English's cricket's structural impasse. Karl Marx may have been referring to the inability of peasant classes to act collectively for their own good when he described them as a sack of potatoes, but were he sitting in the late afternoon sunshine at Lord's today, watching the dying fall of a Division Two Championship game, he might well turn to his neighbour and pronounce, 'Sacks of potatoes, Mr Heffer, that's what them counties are. Sacks of potatoes.' And if he'd read historian Tony Judt, as he probably would have, he'd be aware of Judt's proposition that recent generations 'have made a virtue out of the pursuit of material self-interest'.

Not so long ago there was talk of a new two-division Twenty20 tournament which, for various reasons to do with India, sponsorship, television and county v ECB interests (more of the usual suspects), came to nothing. Before the competition was hoicked down to cow corner, however, and lost in the long grass, someone raised the possibility of marketing the tournament's Division One shirts as a sponsorship package. With central marketing comes the potential to generate more revenue than the counties could aggregate if they were selling their shirt sponsorship individually. I got the impression the idea received short shrift from some counties. Why was that? Self-interest, I guess. Let's, for the sake of argument, say that some bright young blazer at the ECB is able to attract a nine-shirt sponsorship of £1 million. We'll call it a round £110,000 per county and let the ECB pocket the change. You can bet your last copy of *Wisden Cricket Monthly* that at least one county would claim it could get £150,000 for their shirts, so why should they forgo £40,000 to subsidise a less enterprising club? The illustration is hypothetical, yet it corresponds to the real-life collective-bargaining dilemma that America's National Football League faced prior to their 2006 season. Mark Yost précised it as, 'You don't have to compete with my revenues, so don't ask me to share them with you.'

Conscious that the NFL did manage an agreement in the end, I put it to one or two chief executives that some of the smaller counties in particular might benefit from a centralised or collective marketing strategy. I was only flying a kite, and it didn't take long for someone to cut the string.

'There used to be a central marketing of some of the advertising boards at the non-Test match grounds,' Dave Brooks said. 'But when Vodafone pulled out, the whole thing fell apart – just on the back of one sponsor going. It was only £20,000 a year, but that's a young player in your squad basically. I did wonder if they'd really tried hard enough to keep it going. Now the counties have been left to their own devices again, so even that little bit of centralisation fell away fairly quickly.'

In all likelihood those Vodafone ad boards would have been linked to their Team England sponsorship, so it's not as if someone from the ECB had actually gone out selling space on county ad boards. It was no coincidence, after all, that Vodafone's sponsorship of the England team initially coincided with their soon-to-be chairman, Lord MacLaurin, being chairman of the ECB. So the ad boards were little more than a collateral consideration probably; something on the side to keep the smaller grounds sweet. The cynics say that the ECB do that very well.

On the subject of sponsorships, Brooks made an interesting observation drawn as much from his commercial business background as from his more recent experience of cricket administration. 'During the search for a new Sussex sponsor, what we found was that even though cricket was on the one hand quite attractive and relatively cheap, that cheap element also works against it because it's too cheap. Unless you're asking for a million quid, you're taking out most of the major brands. They're not interested in putting in a quarter-million. It's just chicken feed. The other problem cricket faces is that, apart from football and rugby to a lesser extent, everything is a minority sport. Because we approach them as counties we don't really have an appeal to the major national and international brands, and even if we did there are 18 of us so straight away the supply is excessive.'

In 2009 Sussex were one game away from running off with all three limited-overs trophies, and their Sky exposure was ten times greater than the bottom six counties in terms of TV hours. If they found it hard to attract national sponsorship, woe betide anybody else.

For the counties, this perception of being a minority interest has long been a paradox, with the majority of hard-core cricket lovers loath to contemplate it even as a possibility. The nationalistic fervour that has attached itself to the England Test team hasn't helped the counties' cause either. In a way that football doesn't quite manage these days – possibly because England's representatives flaunt a materialism way beyond the reach of their average countryman, or maybe because they're just not good enough – the English cricket team has become an emotional outlet for a nation denied a constitutional identity in the devolutionary carve-up of what has been a united kingdom. Rugby does this as well, and equally as well, but then all four home nations have an on-field identity that approximates to a national extension of local identity.

Cricket's role as national flag bearer feels different, and I can't decide if it's my problem or England's that I'm not comfortable with it. I suspect I worry that Isaiah Berlin knew what he was talking about when he suggested that nationalism may be 'a response to a patronising or disparaging attitude towards the traditional values of a society, the result of wounded pride or a sense of humiliation...' Cricket's support certainly ticks those boxes from what I used to hear around the Test match grounds. I guess I'd be less concerned if I could put all the flag-waving and 'Jerusalem' singing down to high-spirited sporting jingoism. But for some reason I can't. Maybe I should spend more time watching cricket and less time with my head in books. In *The Eclipse of a Great Power: Modern Britain 1870–1975*, Keith Robbins advanced the argument that the English don't need nationalism and do not like it. 'They are so sure of themselves that they need hardly discuss the matter. As one historian recently remarked, "English identity was not in doubt... there was no need to show excessive devotion to St George."'

His flag is much in evidence today, though, and I don't recall it being so back in 1975 when England regrouped under a South African captain, Tony Greig, and held a top-notch Australian team after the first Test was lost with a Scot as captain. England, of course, had David Steele back then and so there was less need for St George. Maybe these days, with South Africans even more in evidence, England's supporters flourish the George to reassure themselves that they are English, even if their team ain't necessarily so. Or it could be that, after centuries of reserve and reservations, they've decided they want to be like other countries and let their national pride hang out. It's not as if they take it to extremes anyway. They don't insist, for example, on driving English cars or taking their holidays in England.

Away from the motorways and the high-density urban traffic, England is a wonderfully therapeutic country to travel around, as green and pleasant a land as the poet imagined. As I discovered while going about the counties, it's better seen sitting in a train than driving the roads, even with the ragtop down and summer's smells on the wind. There are age-old patterns in the greens and new-ploughed browns, the gently rolling downs, the hedgerows and the knots of woodland, the villages passed too soon, the natural and the man-made waterways. Sometimes, to change the eye's focus, a broad sweep of land and an open sky stretch towards a horizon in another county.

You begin to appreciate how the counties differ, red brick giving way to grey stone, tiles replaced by slate, bell towers by steeples, churches by chapels. This is a land that has accommodated difference and change across centuries and generations and it doesn't require a poet's imagination to see how cricket would evolve gradually and naturally here. By the time it reached other countries it was ready made, and yet it was always the English who changed it, bringing in limited-overs formats and Twenty20 frolics as administrators struggled to finance a professional game that had always lived beyond its means, had always lived off other men's means.

Not plugged into music and without a phone on which to tap tap tap my texts and tweets, I thought instead about these counties, their differences and the relationship they had to cricket. How relevant was county cricket to their identity, or had the teams become production-line vehicles with different badges attached to remind exiled sons and daughters where home once was? 'Our feeling flows into places,' Geoffrey Grigson wrote in the introduction to his *Faber Book of Poems and Places*, 'and an accumulation of feeling, historical, cultural and personal, flows back from places into our consciousness.'

I seem to recall one of the poets in this anthology, Edward Thomas, writing that England's roots were in places, and in home as well.

Mark Newton had no doubt what a cricket county meant to its supporters. 'It isn't about convenience of locality and suchlike. For a lot of people it's a lifetime's feeling. We know at Worcester that 40 per cent of our members never attend a game of cricket each year, and I admire that conviction. It's something in their heart, and I believe you see this in cricket more than in other sports. My biggest regret is that I've not supported one team in any sport for life. I wish I had, it's something I miss. I supported Somerset as a kid until I got a job at Surrey and loved going down there regularly for holidays to watch their great players. But how can you support a county you're not working at?' he laughed.

Support can't easily be measured in numbers; membership can. At Taunton, Andy Nash talked of tapping into the Somerset diaspora in order to strengthen their membership numbers. 'When you're competing for the Championship and making finals, support starts waking up all over the place, and we want that support to be an integral part of Somerset County Cricket Club.'

Other counties might want to do the same, for they need the subscriptions as well as the childhood memories and the emotional ties. Only six of the 18 have a membership in excess of 5,000 and all but one of those, Essex, are international grounds where county membership facilitates the purchase of tickets for international cricket. The ECB talk numbers and percentages when it comes to participation in recreational cricket, but we don't hear much from them about fewer than three per cent of the first-class counties' combined population belonging to a county club. There were cheers when county membership rose by almost 3,000 in the wake of the 2005 Ashes, but that was a celebratory blip in a decade that saw some 35,000 members fall by the wayside. They can't all have been bored to death.

'If you take the ECB Financial Report,' Richard Gould said, 'and look at the amount of gate income and membership income from some of the smaller clubs, it is ridiculously low. I find it difficult that in some counties that are located in big cities, where they have 30,000 people watching their football club regularly, and 18,000 watching the rugby regularly, these counties haven't been able to get a bigger slice of the cake. The bigger clubs may look at some of the smaller grounds and say, "Well, you're not pulling your weight commercially because you're not being inventive enough.'"

Tim Lamb also felt some counties could do more to help themselves. 'It somewhat stuck in my craw that counties were nitpicking about how we were managing the affairs of the ECB, notwithstanding substantial hikes in broadcasting income, commercial revenue, etc., when at that stage they were showing little inclination to look to generate money from other sources. I suppose to a certain extent it's the stakeholders' privilege to be able to criticise, but in the time during which the distribution to the counties doubled, in the same period one particular county, I remember, managed to increase the amount of revenue derived from their own efforts by just three per cent.'

Listening to them I almost wondered if they too had been reading Mark Yost's *Tailgating, Sacks, and Salary Caps.* Different ball game of course, on and off the field, but as Yost tells it the owners of big-market NFL teams were never slow to criticise fellow-owners who failed to show the entrepreneurial spirit necessary to maintain a vibrant economical environment for their sport. Not, he noted, that it stopped 'NFL team owners who struggle to sign their own equally lucrative local marketing deals – or prefer to sit back and live off the largesse of the league's revenue-sharing model – from carping the most about an uneven economic playing field.'

Away from the economics of the county game, an area that the clubs have to keep in touch with is cricket's existence as a culture within its communities. It's said that a culture's ability to survive can be gauged from the way it responds to changes within its environment, and the way it responds to the questions asked of its traditions and values. If so, the county game should be able to face the future with a degree of confidence. It may sometimes have been slow to adapt but it has never shown itself averse to catching up with the times. Where it has struggled has been in the willingness, the ability even, of its own cricket community to change with it. This has left the professional game trying to be too many things for not enough people. It has had to spread itself too thinly as it caters for different cricket-watching tastes. It's not as if the game isn't confusing enough for some people without adding to its complexity by introducing different rules for different competitions. England's great strength as a nation may be its ability to absorb and revitalise itself through difference; sport generally moves in the other direction. As the gnarled old pros used to say, keep it simple.

'I think we all acknowledge that Championship cricket is not sustainable,' Gould admitted. 'Everybody has put their hand up and said, the aim of Championship cricket is to create Test match players of the future. There are numbers who enjoy coming to watch it, but there are not enough of them to pay the costs and keep it going. So the only way we can support Championship cricket is through the ECB and through the introduction of a more popular format. We do see a little bit of a clash, I suppose, between the demographics of those who support one in favour of the other, but that clash is getting weaker and weaker all the time. Many more of our members come to watch Twenty20 cricket than they do Championship cricket.'

When it comes to Championship cricket, though, Gould's county is geographically more fortunate than many others, because in cricket terms it covers the waterfronts, drawing support from Devon and Cornwall as well as locally. 'From Bath to Land's End' was how Gould expressed it, and produced a map on his computer to prove it. Just over a fifth of the Somerset membership live in Devon and Cornwall. It can be a good day out to arrive in Taunton early enough for a stroll about the town before the cricket, have lunch in the Long Room Club's swish new dining-room and head off home at close of play after an enjoyable day's cricket. Two and a half to three thousand people would be lost at Headingley, Old Trafford or The Oval, but they make for a good atmosphere at a Championship match in Taunton, and most important of all, the club is again putting a team in the field that's ambitious for trophies.

That said, there's no getting away from the fact that membership has long stopped being the Plimsoll line when it comes to measuring the game's support. Twenty20 has become county cricket's biggest show in town, and in attracting a new audience it has also attracted a different kind of animal. Today's young adult market doesn't much tend towards planning or commitment. Its Twenty20 fan might buy a ticket in advance for a popular fixture but is just as likely to walk up, pay the man on the gate and walk in – to the consternation of those responsible for hiring casual staff, ordering drinks and food, and providing all the services that the average spectators take for granted.

Derby's Keith Loring certainly doesn't like walk-ups. 'I want tickets in hands,' he said emphatically, 'because regardless of the weather, the mother-in-law, the kids, you say, "Sorry, I've got the ticket, I've got to go". But getting tickets in hands means graft, not just advertising in newspapers. It's graft. We'll be at football clubs, giving out fixture cards before the start of the season, we have a partnership with the local university to sell tickets, we have a load of initiatives with the local media.'

But the weather Loring mentioned by way of example has done few favours for advance selling, as David Smith could recall from bitter experience. 'We went into 2007, we pre-sold all our games, and three were completely washed out in that wet June. The result now is that I'd say 50 per cent of our people are walk-ins, whereas what you want in a perfect model are pre-booked. We've gone back to the people who used to book, but don't any more, and offered them a full refund policy to try to get them to pre-book again. But it's a problem. Culturally, if you experience two washouts, you think you'll wait for the day and see what the weather's like. And that's become a risk for all the clubs now.'

Another risk, this time one of the clubs' own making, was their decision to increase for the third time in eight seasons the number of Twenty20 matches. In 2003 and 2004 each county played five preliminary games before the knockout stage; for 2010 and 2011 it was up to 16, or – more to the point – eight home games per county. The snag was that no one knew for certain if the county game had the market to feed this expansion. The cynics had their doubts but who heeds cynics anyhow? Plenty of traditional county members suspected that the counties' eyes were bigger than their audience's stomach for a larger plate of wham-bam batters and dolly dancers, but who ever listened to county members, least of all the traditional kind? You might wonder at the wisdom of going up against the 2010 football World Cup by scheduling all the prelim games in June and July, but this didn't appear to bother anyone I spoke to. The very suggestion that cricket people would stay away because of some football tournament was a heresy met with a sorry look and the sorry comment that time would tell. Well, time tolled its bell and it wasn't a joyous peel.

Some counties made a success of the extended programme, but long before the 2010 competition ran its course there were cries of overkill as grounds failed to fill. Clubs began to call for a reversion to ten games per county, the 2008 and 2009 formula; some wanted the competition scheduled across the season, with a concentration of games on Thursday and Friday evenings instead of the two-month block.

'The rationale for going to 16 T20 matches was that they would be spread over a longer period, but this did not materialise,' Tom Richardson explained. 'Consequently, change now seems inevitable for 2012. What's a pity is that the 16-game format has not been trialled over a couple of months because clearly three or four games a week – playing Essex away on Friday night, for example, getting home at two o'clock in the morning, playing again the next day followed by a break and then a game the following day – is ludicrous. And it demonstrates that the shorter programme is very difficult to make work.'

The few who, like Essex, had 'marketed the hell out of it' vehemently opposed any suggestion of reversionism, although David East did concede that the really successful ones, such as themselves, Somerset and Sussex, had 'bucked the trend by a country mile'.

Others, nevertheless, among them Durham and Northamptonshire, did sufficiently well on corporate selling to compensate in part for the fewer bums on seats. So it wasn't entirely grimmer and gloomier across the board. Indeed it may be that counties will have to look in future to the corporate sector if Twenty20's beer, burps and burger market has found its level.

'With five home games, three of them might have been midweeks,' said Durham's David Harker, 'and so you get three lots of corporate. With eight home games, five of them midweek, you've got five lots of corporate, and the corporate market has been strong for us. Less so the spectator market. Five games, that market picks the three they want to go to. Eight games, they still pick the three they want to go to.'

'We've seen a huge shift in the way that corporate attendances work,' said East. 'The traditional corporate attendance used to be at a Championship match; they'd come along and spend a whole day, taking a leisurely lunch with their clients. That's gone. It's Twenty20 now. It's quick, it's instantaneous and it's outside of business hours. People can justify it and it fits their budgets better. People are really struggling to justify spending six hours at a game of cricket when they're laying people off, so Twenty20 as a product is far more suited to the current business environment.'

What did concern East was that a reduction in the number of games would give the impression that expanding the Twenty20 programme had been a failure. In his opinion it wasn't. Yes, there had been 'a growing momentum which believes that more is less', and to him this seemed perverse. 'If you do something right, then that should be the benchmark aspiration, rather than saying it doesn't work for us so we'll reduce the number to a lower common denominator. Instead of listening to the ones who have failed, why not listen to the ones who've succeeded and find out how they did it?'

Just so, except that communication, cooperation and coordination haven't been cricket's significant C words of late. Conflict, crisis and control are more likely to line up the oranges. What came out of my travels was a conviction that, for county cricket to move forward as a 21st century professional sport, it had first of all to resolve this continuum of conflict, as Matthew Fleming warned at the beginning of the chapter. What made such a resolution appear something of a pipe dream was my impression that conflict was systemic within the administrative structure that services the counties and binds them to the ECB.

Even within each county there is far too much potential for conflict in the relationship between the chairman, the chief executive and, where it still has a constitutional role, the committee. As David East pointed out in Chapter Two, the chief executive is at the coalface of the business, running the operational side. His line of responsibility is to the committee or, in more progressive counties, to a board. The chairman, generally speaking, should be accountable to the county membership whose attention is usually concentrated on what goes on inside the boundary rather than behind it. Members by and large are there for their cricket, not for the cash flow and the balance sheet. And it is the members who vote for the committee and the chairman. So a chief executive struggling to manage his budget can find himself at odds with the members' and chairman's on-field expectations based on the county's sepia-coloured glory days or the promised potential of a young, developing team. The members' desire to retain favourite sons on exaggerated salaries will always be in conflict with the chief executive's need to placate the bank manager or strengthen his commercial team.

While self-interest divides the counties when it comes to politics, policy and business plans, their chief executives do share what East calls 'commonality of purpose'. It is another matter altogether whether their chairmen have this same commonality of purpose, or even a commonality of agenda come to that. They operate to different standards according to ego, personality, business background, position in the community and investment, be it through money or time, in the county. They are, crucially, the members of the ECB and the ones who get to vote there. The chief executives don't even get to be in the same meetings as them. They used to be, in the days of the First-Class Forum, but as we've seen, with something like 50 people sitting around the table, the Forum was unwieldy and unworkable. The way it is now, you can get 18 differing views from the chief executives at their meetings and 18 different views from the chairmen at theirs. Conflicted? That isn't the half of it.

'My chairmen, I've had no idea what they were going to say at meetings,' one chief exec said. 'I'd try to brief them, but at the end of the debate they'd put their hands up and go whichever way they wanted. That's the way it is.'

Not that the county chairmen always get to have the say they want, Neil Davidson explained. There seems to be an awful lot of being told what is happening or going to happen, and not so much deciding what should happen. 'There's a chairmen's meeting two, three times a year and it's a carefully scripted agenda. There's not much time for proper discussion. There was a recall of the chairmen's group a year or so ago to talk about the domestic structure, and that was about the nearest thing in the last three years where the chairmen, who under the constitution are the actual owners of the business, have had some sort of say. Have had some input, other than being liaised with. Basically, the chairmen have been marginalised under this system where there's no formal place for them in the decision-making structure. The only real point of impact they can have is at an AGM and AGMs don't tend to be places where you raise major issues.'

There is no doubt that the ECB like to keep a tight rein on the way they run cricket. If I were to enter 'control' or 'control freakery' in my laptop's Find facility, then browse through my interviews, those words would turn up an uncomfortable number of times for the ECB. Yet as Richard Gould recollected, it's only natural that the Board should have their critics. 'It's easy to kick the headquarters. I was in the army for 12 years and we used to spend a lifetime kicking brigade headquarters or divisional headquarters because they didn't understand what was happening on the ground. Well, that's not always the case; they just have different challenges. I think the ECB do a good job, bearing in mind the breadth of responsibility they have. What I would question is whether those responsibilities are too broad for them to do the best job.'

Others are less complimentary, and don't always bother with the well-spun backhand. Several believed that in recent times the ECB had driven conflict instead of collaboration; that it suited the Board to have weaker counties, because in order to maintain their central control the last thing they wanted was a strong body of counties. As for the Test match grounds taking on the ECB again, it's felt that any challenge to their authority is discouraged by the Board's ability to penalise clubs by withholding major matches. I've even been aware of it myself in writing this book. They say in one-party states that people have two voices, one for inside the house and one for outside, and I was several times saddened to find in county cricket that people thought twice when it came to upsetting the Mao.

What might upset the Board's applecart, however, is the way the pool of international grounds has gone beyond saturation point. Why fear not getting a major match when there are not enough to go around anyway? Far from persuading the big guns to hold their fire, their mutual apprehension could be the catalyst that gives them the courage to step out of line. One day an alternative game plan like the IPL or franchises might look not only tempting but a lifesaver. Just because there has been no breakaway yet doesn't mean some counties won't break ranks when there is something to break away to.

According to Matthew Fleming, this is an interesting time to be involved with cricket in England. But, he adds, 'I've never been involved in an organisation that is successful without a good leader being able to create a clear strategy and deliver it. The constitution of the England and Wales Cricket Board does not enable one man, no matter what the quality of that man, to create a clear strategy that maximises the potential of the game, because that strategy may not be in the interest of the constituent parts. The ECB's greatest chance of success is to make the chairman's role executive, salaried, and to give the board power to make decisions or try to implement decisions that may not necessarily maintain the status quo.'

David East similarly considered leadership of the foremost importance as the counties come to terms with the challenges facing them. 'It's inevitable that there are going to be issues when you're in a competitive environment and working as a cooperative. That's why it needs strong leadership. We've got an ECB board that is constitutionally empowered to take decisions but they still try to do it through consensus and that can't be achieved. So they've either got to row with a very big pair of oars, or we go back to the old system of going round in circles and nothing happening.'

Richard Gould has looked at the way football is structured and wonders if it has anything to offer cricket. Paul and I first spoke to Richard a few months into our research, and some of his ideas returned to us as we tried to gauge answers to two questions that kept coming up during our travels. Where do we want cricket to be in ten years time? How do we get there?

Richard began by outlining the difference between the ECB and football's governing bodies. 'The Football Association looks after the grass roots and the England team, though how long it looks after that, the way it is managed, is I suspect up for debate. You then have the Premiership, which looks after the Premier League, you have the Football League, which looks after all the other league clubs, and you have the Football Foundation, which looks after the grants. So you've got all these different organisations looking after different aspects of the game. Whereas with the ECB you've got one organisation that looks after recreational cricket, domestic professional cricket and international cricket. Sometimes the needs of each bit compromise the needs of the other. It's too much.

'At the very least the ECB should be restructured, and if this was a normal business it would be structured into divisions. You'd have a division for Team England, which would run its own P&L account, and you'd have a division for county cricket, with responsibilities within that division for recreational cricket. It would all sit within a matrix system with a group chief executive if you wanted it, and a group board. Each division might have its own board. At the moment, every decision that is made by the ECB is tempered or compromised by how it might affect the other operations and it doesn't work going forward.'

One reason such a divisional structure hadn't been introduced already, he thought, was because in its absence those in control of the game controlled every part of it. 'And that's probably seen as a nice thing to have.'

Whether it's the best thing for the game is something else entirely. Certainly Richard was not alone in thinking that the time has come for reform of its administrative structure. Stewart Regan, another with experience of football, also looked in that direction for a suitable governance model. 'My view,' he said, 'and I know it's shared by a number of people, is that cricket has to break out as football has, and the ECB has to be split in two. The management of the game and Team England should be distinct from the management of the competitions and the leagues, and within that you can then have a pyramid structure. That would allow at least two boards and two strategies to live in harmony, not in conflict but in partnership. At the moment there's one board which meets once a month, and if you consider the breadth of activity it has to be responsible for, from the rules to the recreational game to the players to the leagues to competitions, to women's cricket, to Team England, how much time on the agenda is each topic allocated in terms of strategic decision-making?

It can't be more than the flick of a switch. There's no time at all to consider fully the detailed requirements to make this game work going forward.

'There is also too much self-interest at present, there are conflicts of interest all the way through. What brought it to a head for me was sitting at a so-called ECB strategy day and the whole day was dominated by Team England. Questions like do we play too much one-day cricket? How do we develop better England cricketers? What can the counties do to help international cricket? The big issues – how do we afford to keep our grounds going, for example, and we're in danger of going bust if we're not careful – these didn't raise a whisper. They didn't even get on the agenda.'

CHAPTER TWELVE
CONVERSATION PIECE

'I don't know whether I buy that or not,' Colin Povey said. 'What you have to have is a governance model that works, haven't you?'

This wasn't the way the conversation was supposed to go. Usually I asked the questions, or offered some half-baked comments, and the person I'd come to see would reply with a reasoned, sometimes cautious, occasionally outspoken answer. Povey was putting the ball back on my side of the court, challenging me to think my statements through. Too much of this and we could end up in one of those Socratic dialogues that Plato loved writing.

It was Jim Cumbes who suggested I talk to Povey. Jim had been telling me how rugby league had become the competition for cricket in the north, now that the game is played in summer and is popular with family audiences. And they were in competition not only for spectators but for column inches.

'We had nobody to compete against before,' he said. 'OK, football at the beginning and end of the season, but in the middle we'd got the whole of the sporting press to ourselves. Now rugby league corners a lot of the market.'

Being a footballer rather than a rugby follower hadn't stopped Jim going along to Sale rugby union club when he was younger, however. But not for the game. 'I used to go with my mates on a Saturday night because they had a disco. They sometimes had a live jazz band on a Sunday as well and it was packed out. Lots of young people there, young women, it was the place to be.'

Well, every club owner knows that if you get the girls in, the guys will follow. It's like bears to the honey jar.

The temptation was to move the talk on to the Old Trafford gigs by the likes of Arctic Monkeys, Take That and Coldplay. Instead we stayed with rugby and, more specifically, rugby as a governance model that cricket might follow. I was wondering if it might offer something different from the structures that Richard Gould and Stewart Regan had outlined. And I was conscious that the Football Association, given its dysfunctional recent past with senior officers coming and going and government ministers calling for reforms, might not seem the obvious example when it came to governance.

Not that the economics of professional rugby stand up to any more scrutiny than professional cricket's. Nor do rugby clubs have to provide international grounds in the way the county cricket clubs have to. Like football, rugby union gets along nicely with one international stadium in London, whereas cricket has always gone on the road, not only in England but in all the Test-playing countries. It takes its contract with its audience more seriously than is often imagined.

What appealed to me about rugby union is the way it restructured itself on embracing professionalism in the mid-1990s. Its various tiers, or divisions, give clubs the facility and flexibility, should they want to exercise either, to move up or down the rugby pyramid without banging their heads against a series of glass ceilings. There is a mechanism, using promotion and relegation, to do something about clubs that settle on the floor above the ceiling and get by on the morsels that drop (if they're lucky) from the rich clubs' table. Clubs find the level and the role that suits them, so historic Richmond, for example, a founder member of both the Football Association and the Rugby Football Union and one of the first rugby union clubs to turn professional, can still flourish several tiers down the pyramid as a non-professional club with some 700 players, fulfilling an essential function in both its local community and in the rugby community.

Dave Brooks reckoned that rugby union was 10 to 15 years ahead of cricket in its professional attitude. There's no disputing that cricket has been insular when it comes to learning from other sports and even from other businesses. There has always been more complacency in cricket than is good for the game. You can sense the frustration felt by chief execs from business backgrounds when they discuss cricket's Neolithic attitude to progress. There are still committeemen who would rather tell a meeting of the time they saw Laker bowl or Compton bat than try to understand the complexities of a balance sheet or the financing of a ground development.

Anyway, that's how I came to be talking to Colin Povey in a Portakabin on the Edgbaston building site. From talking rugby and jazz bands with Jim Cumbes. Nor was I surprised that Colin should be the man to talk to about rugby. He had the physique for engine-room work in a scrum, which just goes to show that you can't rely on first impressions. His sport was water polo. Working for Carlsberg and their sponsorship of sport, however, he'd been involved in most activities from croquet to offshore power-boat racing. He knew his way around the major spectator sports such as cricket, rugby, football and golf and, as mentioned earlier, he was closely involved with Northampton Saints. He found it interesting to be in cricket administration at a time when the game was facing so many big decisions.

'A time when,' he said, warming to this theme, 'the business of cricket has been struggling to find out where it should be. Cricket has been slow to wake up to the commercial operating environment in which an international sport is played. People can argue all they like about how many counties, and the recreational game, and the spread of duties of the ECB, and where MCC fits into all this, but for whatever reason the game of cricket in England has woken up very slowly to the levels of commercialism, professionalism, athleticism and so forth that most major sports have come to expect. In the nicest possible way it's like a village cricket club that's got a bit too big. There are some lovely things about it but there are also some things that in this day and age you have to question.'

When I got him on to rugby, however, Povey didn't draw as distinct a line between the two games as I'd been hoping. 'If you look at the spats that go on fairly frequently between the RFU, England, Premier Rugby and individual Premier rugby clubs – just cross out rugby and put in cricket really, whether it's central contracts, England player availability, burn-out or international scheduling. Added to which, cricket and rugby are also similar in that they both provide a safe environment for all the family.

'But what you get with the duration of cricket games, unfortunately, is an uncomfortable fit with modern life and modern society. My son will be at home tonight, and he'll probably have a cricket game on his laptop. He'll play a five-day Test match in 15 minutes; he'll have scored more runs than Kevin Pietersen and thrashed Australia again in the blink of an eye. My point is that the ability of family groups and many people to come and watch traditional four- and five-day cricket is difficult in this modern age.'

What English cricket requires, Povey contended, is a proper strategy – as opposed to a string of public relations mantras – for what and where cricket should be. Which is how I came to say that I'd been struck by the extent to which so many counties appeared to be in the game for themselves, protecting their own interests ahead of those of the game as a whole. Perhaps I'd been taking too much interest in the playing side when I was working in cricket regularly, but I hadn't been conscious of the counties, be they Test match grounds or the smaller clubs, looking over their shoulder all the time in case another county stole a march. To my way of thinking, this constant suspicion put the counties in a position of weakness at a time when they should be working together from a position of strength. Didn't this leave them vulnerable to manipulation by the ECB? Wasn't it time, I suggested, for the counties to consider the reform of the game's governance structure? They were the owners, or so everyone kept telling me.

Which is when Colin Povey volleyed my question back over the net. 'I don't know whether I buy that or not. What you have to have is a governance model that works, haven't you?'

Did that sound as if he thought the current one did work? Birmingham's a fun city to visit, but I hadn't gone there to hear that cricket's governance was hunky-dory. I could visit an art gallery, go to a restaurant or get a ticket for a concert.

'Why would you say it doesn't work?' he asked. 'If I'm sat at the centre, England have got the Ashes, they've won a world cup for the first time.'

But that's just part of the story, I argued. The Ian MacLaurin successful shop window theory. Get a winning England team and the rest will follow. I had no quarrel with that. My argument, if I was fighting the counties' corner, which I hoped I was, was that the shop window had become the whole marketplace. I have a feeling that Plato never let Socrates near the marketplace, but we'll skateboard around that.

'Maybe it is the marketplace,' Povey replied. 'I'm only arguing as the guy at the centre. Whether I believe it or not is another matter.'

Thank goodness for that. So let's agree that the shop window has become the marketplace. Team England is the only show in town. Why do we need as many as 18 suppliers to produce the product?

'You may not do, but you wouldn't get 18 county chairmen to say that. It might mean one of them would lose his first-class status.'

There's no disputing that. Old Socrates may have known his hour was up, but you go your way and I'll go mine wasn't going to be the call around the counties just yet. So, I suggested to Povey, because I was getting the hang of this disputatious lark, let's say you're still at the centre, you're the ECB. You've got this wonderful product that is Team England, you're winning lots of games, you're on television virtually all summer with the best cricketers playing high-intensity cricket. That's your brand. It stands up well against its football and rugby equivalents because it's a winning brand.

Nike, a winning brand if ever there was, decided if I remember rightly that they didn't need to manufacture their products. They only needed to buy them in from outside suppliers and then market them. Same with the IPL, come to think of it. The franchises buy in players from around the world. What we have here, however, is a successful brand, Team England, and it's produced by 18 factories that cost a lot of money to run.

'And, you might argue, factories that don't produce enough because some of that winning team is currently made up of players born or developed elsewhere. Right now it's South Africa but it could be somewhere else next year.'

Setting that argument to one side, there are still 18 by however many people producing goods that could be produced by half that number.

'Correct,' said Povey. 'But then you have an obligation to your shareholders, your constituent members. Equally, I would argue, if I was at the centre, look at the growth in recreational participation. The grass roots of the game are in rude health. Look how much money we've invested in player participation so that the pool is getting bigger. Now you might argue that we've got too many A roads and not enough motorways, not enough high-speed lines but plenty of track, or whatever the equivalent is, but I think if you sat at the centre you could say, "Actually, guys, overall we're delivering for you, aren't we?"'

But what about my factories? The guys at the grass roots, the recreational players, they're OK for the time being. It's the 18 counties that are the point of concern. That's the construct that has its critics. Povey has an answer to that as well. 'Can you envisage any ECB chairman standing on a mandate that says, "I'll tell you what, we should have 12 counties instead of 18?" He'd never get in.'

He's right, of course. The usual suspects can huff and puff to their lungs' content but they'll not bring the house down. Not yet. I see Shane Warne has joined the gang, saying it's time to cut county cricket from 18 teams to 10. Maybe that's his doosra. I'll stay with my Pauline thesis and attempt to show that 18 counties are sustainable because they provide value beyond the cricket field. So I put my

Richmond theory to Povey. No longer in the top flight professionally but still successful as a sports club, could Richmond not be a model that some counties could adopt in the future?

'It might have to be,' he agreed. 'But my argument is that the governing body of that organisation, the Rugby Union, eventually facilitated and led that change. They set their stall out to manage the transition, and what you had for a period was huge risk and no little chaos at club level. At the top end of the sport you had investors who bought in, took huge personal risks and most of them have seen no return whatsoever for that investment and risk. And however bloody and difficult the dialogues, the negotiations and discussions were, the RFU worked through that transition.

'If you look at football and the emergence of the Premier League, you can't think for a minute that that was an easy set of conversations for the FA and the Football League and the Premier League to go through. But at the end of the day you still have the FA, you have the Premier League, you have the Championship, and you have a workable structure.

'What you didn't have, ultimately, in those instances was governing bodies treating all of the clubs as the same. So in rugby the way in which Leicester Tigers managed to survive, to be successful and get rewarded, was very different from London Scottish and Richmond down the line. At one stage those clubs would all have been on a par. Having had that period of turmoil and change, Leicester Tigers will be getting paid a lot more money by the RFU, because of the players they produce, than London Scottish or Richmond or whoever. And people have found, and organisations have found, their level in that revised structure under the retained governance of the RFU, the governing body.

'But the governing bodies in those instances, I would argue, were more proactive about dictating or working towards a new structure – as opposed to saying, "We can't change anything so we'll just stay where we are." Which is where cricket is at the moment.

The financial opportunities as perceived by the rugby clubs were also probably greater than in cricket, and this must have a bearing on our current position.

'Does everybody agree that we play too much cricket and need a sensibly scheduled domestic calendar? Yes we do. Why can that not be solved then? I have no idea, but there must be a solution. If you look at the economics of the commercial, professional game, it doesn't make great sense in terms of the numbers of competitions and structures and counties that we currently have. But at present we do not yet have enough collective leadership or commercial pressure to lead ourselves to a new promised land.'

So maybe the counties should be having the kind of conversation we were having, however problematic it might be to formulate a common agenda for such a fragmented group.

'As the game becomes more commercialised,' Povey said, 'as some of the other problems are fixed, then there will be more time to debate these sort of subjects, I'm sure.'

But not now?

'If you went to a meeting of 18 county chief executives and said, "Hands up those who think cricket's a good idea," you'd probably get 18 hands go up, but beyond that, who knows. Ask them any other question and you probably wouldn't get 18 hands going up together. The difference between, pick any one you like, I'll pick Northampton because I live over that way. Ask Northampton about their cricket and ask Surrey about their cricket. They're not even in the same universe, let alone the same planet or postcode. If you were to ask Warwickshire about their position relative to Lord's and MCC, we're a completely different proposition altogether.'

Povey looked at his watch and finished whatever he was drinking. We'd been talking for more than an hour all told, going over a range of subjects, and there was a major development outside that required his attention. I thanked him for his time and was leaning across the desk to turn off the recorder when he looked up from the papers he was gathering and offered a final thought. 'One of the things about sport is that it's an emotional thing, and in a lot of sports emotion over-rules everything else for a lot of the time. That makes it a dangerous business environment to be in. In all sports, and cricket is no better or no worse, you see emotion taking over from an objective assessment of the facts. It's very difficult in a sporting environment to get a rational, logical, long-term plan mapped out because there's just too much emotion around. What's a crisis in sport? Lose three on the bounce in football and it's carnage for managers. Look how many cricket captains have gone this last year. Eight, including our own. That's almost half the field, and chief execs have been leaving also.

'In the middle of all this, however, we have to remember we've got a product that has great appeal when we get it right. It's an international product, and if we can get a virtuous circle around the emotion and the business of sport, it's a very healthy space to be in.'

As ifs go, that sounded about as positive as it gets.

CHAPTER THIRTEEN
VILIA MIRETUR VULGUS

How many years did Dave Brooks say cricket was behind rugby union? Ten to 15? Nothing to speak of really when you consider it was some 80 years behind Dada. It was around 1922 when Hans Arp, one of the movement's progenitors, came up with a game that used planks instead of bats and raw eggs for balls. The game was all about humiliating its players. The ECB didn't go quite that far when they brought in Twenty20, although in the eyes of traditional cricket lovers they did humiliate the game somewhat. In defence of Twenty20, however, and with a nod in the direction of Francis Ford Coppola and Robert Duval, I do love the sight of cellulite and hot pants first thing in the evening.

It did, however, take me time to get the format into context. After all, when you've been within target range of a Viv Richards Exocet clearing extra cover like some bad moon rising, or sampled dolly mixtures at the Whisky a Go Go, Twenty20 doesn't have too much special going for it. What it really has is social significance. That slew of six-greeting ghetto-blasting, the franchise to elevate county cricket's interminable mediocrity to the terminally mundane, the television screen in the corner: cricket has twinned the vernacular of modern living with the vulgarity of everyday street life. No wonder it draws a crowd. Even Ovid foretold it would when he wrote, in Latin naturally, 'Let the trash amuse the masses; I'll settle for the full jar that golden boy Apollo pulls down at the Castalian.'

We've been hearing how the expansion of Twenty20 in 2010 took the format from boom to bust at some counties. Bust enough certainly for loud cries to reduce the number of games, and bust enough for the ECB to respond with that well-known cricket cure-all, a working party. Two meetings, that's all it took, for the working party to come up with a proposal for 2012 that would not only see a return to ten games each at the Twenty20 preliminary stage but also reduce the number of County Championship fixtures from 16 to 14 per county. For a while now there'd been approaches from the players and the Team England mafia for a shorter county programme, as recommended by the 2007 Schofield Review of the England team following the previous winter's Ashes debacle in Australia. The belief was that less cricket would allow the players more time during the season for meaningful preparation, conditioning and skills-based practice. More time on the golf course, muttered the cynics among the county members.

The clubs, meanwhile, looked to the reduction in games as a means towards reducing fixture congestion and the physical drain of the travel that went with it. 'On the last 30 days of the season,' said Somerset chairman Andy Nash, 'our cricketers played on 23 of them. That's patently absurd.'

He didn't mention, but could have, that Somerset were also in contention for the 2010 Championship and CB40 titles throughout that month and, having earlier reached the Twenty20 finals, were probably patently knackered. They'd been on a long, hard and possibly even winding road since mid-April. Not that they were alone in this. Colin Povey's illustration from Warwickshire's season was mirrored at every county. 'Our guys had a run of 12 days play out of 14 in the middle of the summer. We went Friday night here at Edgbaston in the T20, Sunday another T20 at Trent Bridge, off to Durham that night, played them in a four-day Championship game followed by a T20 on Friday then back on the bus down to Yorkshire for a T20 on Sunday and a Championship game starting Monday morning. It's just a nonsense by way of a schedule for either players or fans. It can't be good for the quality of the game we put on for our domestic spectators.'

It would be all too easy to blame the people who have to put the fixture list together. Kicking a man when he's down would be kinder. Alan Fordham, who heads up the ECB's First-Class Operations section, the FCO, has a thankless task when it comes to arranging the season's schedule.

'It's like trying to put a quart into a pint pot,' David East sympathised. 'There are commercial pressures, there are cricketing pressures, there are travelling pressures, unavailability pressures in terms of grounds, festivals, the broadcasting agreement. There are a huge number of different and conflicting parameters that Alan has to juggle with, so I think he does a really good job of trying to give us as much as he can within the constraints he has. I wouldn't criticise anyone who sorts the scheduling out operationally.

'What's more to the point is that we have to make a conscious decision about what we're playing and when we're playing it. There are lots of different views on that, and this is the difficulty we face. I've been around quite a long while now, and there are others who've been around longer. David Acfield [Essex off-spinner and committeeman] and I, together we've been through about ten Domestic Structure Reviews, and you keep going round in circles because ultimately one group will want something different from another group. So someone has either got to say we're going to do this by consensus – in other words we're never going to make a significant change – or someone has to have enough balls to actually make a decision and say to hell with you all, this is the way it's going to be. And that's the conflict we've got.'

Oh dear, that word conflict again, but hardly unexpected when, as Tom Richardson sighs, 'We can't accept the fact that we agreed a programme and that's what we're going to do for another four years.'

The programme he was talking of was the one agreed in 2009. We'll leave aside for the time being what the counties had decided in 2008 for seasons 2010 to 2013. In 2009, for those same four years, they voted 13-5 for a structure that would comprise a 16-match, two-division Championship, a Twenty20 competition and a 21-team 40-overs Sunday afternoon competition in three pools.

'There was a lot of flapping about over that,' Tom went on, 'but it was the right decision. We'd keep the Championship at 16 games and drop one competition, the 50 overs. We want Twenty20, we want 40 overs, and having trialled this for a year the 40 overs continued to be well supported in the second half of the year. Crowds were sparse in April and May but perhaps that's no surprise.'

It certainly seems that 40 overs are what the punters want. The 50-over game is just too long in this day and age. Those 20 overs saved make all the difference between a day-long commitment and an afternoon's cricket, as Andy Nash pointed out. 'We prefer the 40 because it's more digestible. We can get six, seven thousand at Taunton for the 40-over games. There's a considerable body of members who will say that T20's great but it's all over too quickly. They like to take a good half-day over their cricket.'

What concerned Dave Brooks about the 40-over game was not its length so much as the way it was being marketed. There was a danger, he thought, of making it appear too similar to Twenty20. 'When you look at the people who come to watch 40-over cricket, most of them are old enough to remember the John Player League and they're like me, they loved that. So I think if you market 40-over cricket too much as Twenty20's bigger brother, rather than as a faster-paced County Championship, there's a risk that you'll disenfranchise some of the members who prefer 40-over cricket. It's a middle product that moves people from four-day cricket to Twenty20 cricket or vice versa, or allows people to meet in the middle. You've got to be careful not to push it too far one way or the other. Does that mean it's a bit of a compromise? I don't think that's too bad.'

If anything, it would seem that the 40-over game, by keeping its head down and going about its business, has remained something of an unsung success, a bit of a hybrid maybe but none the worse for that in a country coming to terms with coalition government and parliamentary compromise. It's the siblings either side that give the parents sleepless nights when they're not hung over from yet another working party. They do seem to like their partying at the ECB, and why not? Working parties give the suits another set of meetings to chair and minutes to circulate, so justifying their salaries. They provide the *Daily Telegraph*'s mole with inside information to leak, and they send the counties scooting back to their corners to dust down their vested interests before they come out fighting again.

Getting everybody to sit down and agree the right answers for the game has always tried and tested cricket administrators, from the heady affairs of the ICC to village green fixture lists. And heaven knows the structure suggested at the end of 2010 for the 2012 county season couldn't have been better designed to get the counties up in arms if someone had actually set out to foment contention. Not so much the reduction of games perhaps, but the way the Championship would be restructured with eight counties in Division One and ten in Division Two. The Division One teams would play each other twice; the Division Two teams would play each other once and only some teams twice, a reversion to the asymmetrical system used before the full implementation of four-day cricket in 1993. If the impression hadn't already existed that the Division Two counties were virtually second-class citizens, it would now. So, having begun the season with the threat of secession, the game was ending the year with a proposed structure that could lead to civil war. No one was yet admitting that there were too many counties, but the message coming out of the muddle seemed clear enough. There were too many counties within the fixture schedule and the formats that county cricket was struggling to sustain.

It brought to mind a radical suggestion that someone made along the way, albeit insisting that it was off the record. I could hardly blame him for the proviso. One of the more interesting questions, he volunteered, is whether you need the same number of counties for Championship cricket and for one-day and Twenty20 cricket. There was an argument, he thought, for saying to some counties, why don't you just focus on the shorter formats? Forget the four-day game.

Reading about the proposed changes to the playing structure – in the *Telegraph* of course; where else? – reminded me of a long conversation I had with Dave Brooks at Hove on Election Day. Brighton was buzzing with expectation that Caroline Lucas would become the Green Party's first MP at Westminster, the TV camera crews were getting ready for the count, St George's flag was at full stretch above the Grand Hotel, and a few pensioners, wrapped against the wind, raised their winter complexions to the sub-par sun. There were a few more pensioners at the County Ground, cluttered around the north end in a cliché of deck chairs, and the car park was full. Apart from the floodlights nothing much had changed since the Saturday morning Viv Richards launched his aerial assault on the press box. It wasn't so much going back in time as time standing still. 'Change is inevitable,' American trade union activist and Obama supporter Andy Stern liked to say, 'progress is optional.' He'd have felt at home at Hove.

'The fixture list for 2010 was always going to be the straw that broke the camel's back,' Brooks said. 'A year ago, 2009, 16 counties wanted to retain 16 first-class fixtures, symmetrical, Division One, Division Two. One wanted to go back to all playing each other once, 17 games, and one basically couldn't give a toss about four-day cricket and would happily have played Twenty20 and one-day cricket and probably not bothered with the Championship. I always felt that it was only a matter of time before the majority position was no longer sustainable, particularly given the pressure to end the season earlier so that counties can take part in the Champions League. I believe it's good for English cricket to be involved in international club competition, so that's a compromise we should be prepared to make. We should work very positively with the Champions League to ensure that the tournament is played in the third and fourth week of September so we can go, even if it does mean we are a bit under-cooked and not fully prepared for it. That, however, puts some pressure on the season.

'The other thing that has left us stymied is that we kicked off too early this year. It's almost as if, "Look guys, you voted for 16 Championship games and this is the result." It's just not sustainable. Starting on 9 April was bonkers. We'd played four Championship games by the end of April, we're in the first week of May and this is our fifth. It's too early to start, but given that we don't want to extend the season through to the end of September we had to start that early to fit all the games in. And even then it's too congested. There are 90 days out of 160 this year when we're playing cricket, let alone the travel time. You can pretty much forget about any real rest and recuperation time or periods of reflection. It's just a treadmill.

'So we've got 18 counties all unanimously saying this can't go on. We can't get any agreement on what the appropriate structure is going forward, but everyone's saying what we've got is not sustainable. Which has created significant issues already, because going into this season we still didn't know what the structure of county cricket was going to be for 2011. So would we be playing for promotion and relegation this year or not? If not, why am I spending tens of thousands of pounds on an overseas player? We can't go up, what's the point; we can't go down, what's the point? You may as well take it to its most irrelevant extreme, bank the age-related performance fee payments and then splash out next year when the format's decided. It was a crazy position to be in with the season two weeks away.

'But that's the problem we have with the governance structure we've got. We can't make a decision quickly enough. What we need is for the ECB, as the leader of the sport, to come out and say, "Boom, this is what's happening. There's going to be a review and it will be implemented in 2012 so, sorry, you've got a horrible season ahead of you and another bad one coming up in a year's time. However, we'll implement the new one in 2012. We don't yet know what it's going to look like, but given it's going to reduce the amount of Championship cricket it might have an impact on promotion and relegation. We'll let you know by such and such a date. But because we have to go through this consultation process…"'

Brooks threw out his hands in despair.

'Where we are, we have to get to probably 12 games in the Championship, because all 14 does is allow you to start two weeks later and still have the same congested period. We know the England team management favour promotion and relegation; I suspect most county coaches don't because it doesn't give them the opportunity to develop young players, particularly in Division One. We were making decisions last year [2009] to be playing someone like Jason Lewry when we should have been playing a 23- or 24-year-old seamer. But we couldn't do that because we were battling to stay up.

'A conference structure? I don't see how it gets you to 12 games, because all the plans I've seen have you playing 12 games and then a play-off. So you may end up with 14 games anyway. I don't know what the solution is really. I'm not against the divisions being of different sizes, with Division One being the smaller, playing home and away matches still, while in Division Two you accept you play each other once and a couple of people twice. It wouldn't be the end of the world.'

That night Caroline Lucas broke the mould and won herself a seat. For a betting man, or woman, her victory was a safer bet than putting money on the counties to get their house in order. The only thing that could be said with any confidence was that discontent was bubbling to the boil quite nicely around the grounds in the aftermath of the Champions League snub by the IPL, the fall-out from the abortive franchise expedition to India and the fixture list farrago. No one was short of something to say and generally speaking they didn't hold back on saying it.

A Somerset member probably spoke for county members across the country when he said that 'English cricket has lost its rhythm'. Andy Nash agreed and said he couldn't have put it better himself.

'That's what we need to get back. You need to know it's Championship cricket on hopefully Monday to Thursday, Friday night is T20 and on Sunday you've got 40 overs. Right now people don't know where they are.'

He's spot on about that. Even people in the game are struggling to know what's going off out there, as Fred Trueman used to explode on *Test Match Special*, back in the days before it rebranded itself as *TMS*.

'I pick a paper up in the morning,' Jim Cumbes said, 'and I'll look at a scorecard and think, is that the first day or the second? Unless it actually says second day of four, I won't know for sure because I can then look at another scorecard and hey, it's the first day, that one. So if I'm looking at the paper and wondering what day it is, what about the ordinary guy? I know what our games are but I don't know what somebody else's is. We always used to know with three-day cricket. Saturday start, Monday, Tuesday, Wednesday start, Thursday, Friday. OK, we know that's moved on, but members miss it, the rhythm of it. They come up and ask why they don't get county cricket over the weekend. Occasionally there is,' he chuckled, 'and nobody comes. They've got out of the habit.

'Years and years ago, when your three-day game would start on a Saturday, we might get three or four thousand people here at Old Trafford before lunch. By the time you got to the afternoon, half of them might have gone, disappeared up to the leagues. They'd watch county cricket in the morning and league cricket in the afternoon.'

As Jim said, those were different times, and as Keith Loring reminded me, cricket was a different market for an audience back then. 'Since you and I began watching sport, say 40 years ago, every single year something else has happened. Joe Public didn't play golf 40 years ago. Men go shopping on Saturdays with the wife or family today. The choices are enormous. And another thing, for parents with kids the amount of work they have to do with them these days. Kids don't go out and play any more. Everything's organised. By the time the parents have done all that, they haven't got time for some of the things they used to do. It's not surprising they sit down in front of the television with all the choice and channels on offer these days. And we're having to compete with that change in society as well.'

Whether or not the way to meet the competition is to reduce the amount of cricket on offer is something else. Mark Newton, no longer working in the game, found it extraordinary that cricket would want to go down that route. 'The most prosperous models around the world of sport are about playing,' he argued. 'Baseball play something like 160-odd games a year; effectively they play two games a day in many of their arenas. They have two different squads, with three or four pitchers on the roster. NBA is 82 games now. American football, while it's only once a week, has extended its season by two weeks. Ice hockey play three or four times a week. The players must be knackered but they just get out there and do it because they're earning good money. And on top of that there's the travel, but that's the job. They're professional sportsmen. I fail to understand the arguments in cricket sometimes, except of course it's the classic cricket versus commercial.

'If the best sports models are those whereby everybody wins – spectators have low prices, the best stadiums and the best spectacle, the players are the best paid in the world – why are we not following that commercial model? People moan about the number of games in the Premier League, but the reason the players get so much money, and generally speaking everybody is happy with the product, is because it's played regularly and often. There are so many fallacies about sport,' he sighed before continuing.

'They talk about going down to 12 Championship games. That means going down to six home games, which means you're disen-franchising one of your core revenues, the membership. We know it will happen eventually, but I hope we'll make up for it by playing other cricket at other times. However, there's a much deeper philo-sophical discussion, isn't there. How important is four-day cricket? What are we trying to achieve in future years? What is the product?

'This comes back to something you raised earlier about the balance of tradition with the modern. I went through that with rugby league, and you don't get anything more fundamental than the move from winter to summer. I remember the day we launched it, and the reaction to it was horrendous. Yet within three or four years it was a highly successful club product. Crowds were up. You went to watch a game on a nice warm day instead of in the snow and the sleet, and all those feelings of lost traditions rapidly disappeared. We've got to go through that same transition in cricket. The problem we have is that we're trying to be the best to all, so the leap we have to make is going to be very difficult.'

'There's a reluctance to repackage cricket in a way that fits the modern age,' Paul Millman said. 'The parallel I draw is with Lucozade. Lucozade used to be a product beside hospital beds for grannies. The owners were able to repackage it as Lucozade Sport and it's become a brand leader. The trouble with cricket is we're holding on to the old grannies-bed model. We haven't had the courage to repackage it in a relevant way.'

Perhaps that's the problem generally. There aren't enough strong, authentic brands in cricket to hold the public's attention, let alone their affection.

'I don't want to be the one who says, four-day cricket, forget about it at county level,' Mark Newton replied. 'I want a peaceful retirement when it comes. But somebody has to say it before long. Nor is three days the answer; it's still too long for a modern audience. Why would somebody with a young family give up a whole day to watch the first day of a three-day spectacle? You don't go to the theatre or cinema or a football match to watch a third of it or a half of it and go back the next day. It's not in the psyche. The only game I can think of worldwide that has similarities would be golf, where tournaments are played over four days. But that has a different style and a different momentum.'

Just in case you're getting the impression that Newton is some dangerous radical like those well-known usual suspects Willis, Wright,

Chappell and Atherton, the impression I got was of someone who is anything but. A moderniser, yes, but that was because he cared passionately about sport, loved thinking and talking about it. When it comes to Test cricket, for instance, he would even describe himself as a traditionalist. 'I love watching Test cricket,' he said. 'I go every holiday to watch Test matches abroad, but I don't get the same feeling from four-day county cricket. What Twenty20 is delivering to Test cricket is a lot more excitement at last. I grew up in the sixties: two runs an over in a day was exciting. Now, if batsmen don't score at three and a half, four runs an over, Test cricket is boring. Maintaining that excitement is the only way we'll get people to watch five-day cricket in big numbers. Whether players will take a Twenty20 approach to four-day cricket, though', he shrugged, 'I don't know.

'You go back to when one-day cricket first came into county cricket. If you had to score six runs an over you were going to struggle to win. Today, six runs an over in any form of one-day cricket is a cakewalk. Shot-making ability is innovative; bowlers are getting better. If anybody says to me that cricket is not as it used to be, that skills aren't as they used to be – skill sets now are infinitely better than they were in the so-called good old days. What batsmen are doing now with their shot-making is phenomenal. What bowlers are having to learn from Twenty20 is phenomenal. What fielders are doing is phenomenal. Cricket's a highly skilled game compared to where it was 10, 15, 20 years ago, whatever anyone says. So four runs an over in a Test match now and we stroll it, and the reason we stroll it is because batsmen are actually doing what the game is all about. Just like baseball, they're trying to hit the ball out of the ground, and that's what brings the high reward.'

To find unequivocal support for the four-day game, more accurately for the Championship game, I knew I wouldn't have to go further than Grace Road and David Smith, and he didn't let me down. As with Mark Newton, his passion for cricket is evident in every word he utters, and he certainly doesn't believe the four-day game has no place in county cricket. 'We get a lot of chief execs, who I call the new breed of chief execs, who look down their noses at Championship cricket. The fact is it has a massive following. It's not just about who is in the ground, it's the Internet that I'm flicking on at the moment and following the scores of the counties that are playing. A lot of business people do that all over the UK. If you look at the hits on sites like CricInfo, BBC Cricket, Test Match Extra, they're huge for Championship cricket.'

Just how huge all this Internetting is for productivity in the UK workplace might also be worth consideration, but maybe that's just me showing my Stakhanovite side, which the *Daily Telegraph* once told its readers I possessed. Fortunately I had a good dictionary to hand at the time. But back to David Smith.

'Yes, there are a number of people who pay their membership sub and don't go that often to Championship cricket, but they feel part of the club and want to support the club financially wherever they can. I think a lot of the newer chief execs struggle to understand that, and that's because they look at bums on seats and then wonder why they're doing it because they're not making any money. But actually cricket and money, unlike other sports, it's a very, very different game.'

Like a lot of the people I spoke to, Smith did think that in the longer term county cricket would be just two formats, the Championship and Twenty20. 'I'd hate to put a time frame on it,' he said, 'but I think it's inevitable that that's where we'll end up. If you said to the average chief executive you'll have a Twenty20 game every second Sunday throughout the season, they'd probably go for that.'

Given that the Schofield Review in 2007 had recommended that domestic formats should 'as far as possible mirror the international game', and indeed a year later, after one of those Domestic Structure Review thingies, the ECB had agreed to drop 40 overs and keep 50, it is evident that, come getting down and dirty time, the commercial interests get their way as often as not. The counties kept 40 overs and dropped 50. Not that domestic 50 overs has been the pathway to

World Cup success for England. It wasn't even a flicker on the English landscape for all that long, having been adopted as late as 1996, nine years after becoming the World Cup format.

To be honest, if the international game were the sole criterion for a 50-over competition, England would have been better off doing what they do in the longer form of the game. Put the best cricketers on central contracts and into boot camp. It's been a proven formula in bridging the gap between Championship cricket and Test cricket; there's no reason why it can't work for one-day cricket.

However, I'm not suggesting the County Championship should go the way of 50 overs, although I have heard the conspiracy theorists express the view that the ECB believe Championship cricket is no longer the core of the English game; that their central academy could provide the talent needed for a successful England team without the Board having to maintain the Championship. It's not a thesis that David East for one would subscribe to, even though he has no illusions about Championship cricket's role in the master plan.

'You can dress Championship cricket up as much as you want, but while it's a prestigious tournament we all want to win, ultimately it's a development game. It's not sustainable as a stand-alone competition and we know that, we've accepted that, so we're saying that it's an important part of the process for our game's business model. We get paid for it through the money coming down from the centre. We're doing it through our academies, through our development infrastructure; it's a virtuous pyramid. We work at the grass-roots level with our Emerging Player programmes through the county boards, through the county club academies and into first-class cricket. The next step up is into the international teams, and we're four-square behind that concept.'

Stewart Regan sounded similarly pragmatic about Championship cricket's place in the bigger picture, but after listening to him you might decide he made the right move when he left Yorkshire for the bracing winds of Scottish football and its revolting referees. There was probably too much of the practical businessman about him for average cricket tastes. For one thing he looked to the future rather than the past.

'If you were to ask what we all want,' he said, 'we all want to see full grounds, we all want to see new entrants into cricket – kids, families, the Asian community in our case – and at the moment we're in a situation where we've got four-day cricket, Test cricket and one-day cricket and it doesn't really pay for itself. You take the cost of four-day cricket. How much it costs to put a team up for four days in a hotel, the cost of transporting them around the country, the cost of stewarding a game and cleaning the ground, when you're getting like twopence halfpenny coming through the turnstiles. Even when you amortise your membership revenue across the season it doesn't pay for itself. The way you have to view four-day cricket is that, in rugby terms, we're England Reserves; four-day cricket is England Reserves. We're getting paid by England out of the TV revenue to develop future England players.'

In which case why not simply open the gates and let people come in and watch? Why make them pay to watch a development game? Who knows, you might even attract a crowd. It might give tomorrow's England heroes experience of playing staid old first-class cricket in front of a decent house without the customary Twenty20 clamour.

'I think there is a short-term view on that and a long-term view,' Regan answered. 'The short-term view is that there are still a lot of club members around the country who thrive on the four-day game. If you look at Yorkshire's membership, we have 8,500 members. I would guess that about 80 per cent, if not more, are members because they love the four-day game. Now if you projected that five years hence, I would say that with members dying off and not being replaced by lovers of the four-day game, they'll be replaced by Twenty20 season-ticket holders rather than members. Members clubs will eventually be replaced by plcs, no longer Industrial and Provident Societies but companies à la Manchester United, Aston Villa and so forth. That way we'll see an evolution in cricket. There'll still be four-day cricket, because players still need something to develop their skills, they still need to learn how to be Test cricketers, but I don't think people will worry that much about attendances at the four-day game. The attendance focus will be on Twenty20.'

CHAPTER FOURTEEN
'WE NEED A CHAMPION'

'Don't put all your money on Twenty20 being that focus. We should be very careful about its future,' warns the Professional Cricketers' Association's Angus Porter. 'People have set out a huge amount of stall on the demand for T20, and assumed the media market for it is limitless. I don't think we can assume that is correct.'

I'm inclined to agree with him. County cricket in England has arrived at a point where it is difficult to forecast where it's headed. It could stay on the road along which it's been travelling, not doing anything too adventurous, getting by on the reassurance of familiar formats as it keeps on rolling, Mississippi style, from crisis to crisis, survival to survival, good times to bad and back again. No wonder people say that cricket reflects life. It could, however, take the turning that veers off to the side, staying in sight of the original road until that gradually slips from view and a new but not too different horizon beckons. We could call that evolution road. Or it could hang a hard left and create a new-look highway that leaves the old ways behind. Not necessarily a revolutionary road but certainly something radical.

Meanwhile, we're still standing here at the crossroads and there's also the option of selling cricket's soul to the devil. It wouldn't be the first time or the last, merely the latest. Why is it that whenever I hear the folk duo Show of Hands sing 'Is there anything left in England that's not for sale?' I think immediately of Lord's, Allen Stanford's helicopter and ECB suits salivating over the Texan millionaire's open container of dubious dosh?

'This royal throne of kings, this sceptred isle,' begins Shakespeare's John of Gaunt, flattering his audience further with 'This other Eden, demi-paradise', teasing the listener this way and that like Shane Warne measuring up a new victim and then finishing him off with that faster, flatter flipper. 'This land of such dear souls, this dear dear land, is now leas'd out ... like to a tenement or pelting farm. England ... is now bound in with shame, with inky blots and rotten parchment bonds; That England, that was wont to conquer others, hath made a shameful conquest of itself.' At least Robert Johnson got to play great blues guitar in return for his soul. The endgame for the counties, whether their souls are sold for Texan swag or Sky silver, is that they get to play nothing more than second fiddle to the England team. Become Stewart Regan's 'England Reserves' in fact, a scenario that is contingent with downsides.

One is that four-day cricket's audience will eventually say enough is enough. 'You're expecting us to watch a trial match for possible England players. Well, we're not interested in that.' Linked to this is the longer-term risk of undermining the spectator base for England games. As David Harker asks, 'If the focus of the English game really is Test cricket, what happens to the audience for Test cricket if there's no longer interest in the longer form just beneath that? Are we playing so much international cricket that the Test match can exist entirely on its own?'

Should the answer be no, then the challenge for the ECB and the counties is to market the Championship game as one not just for members but for everyone with an interest in cricket. Harker agrees with what David Smith said earlier about there being sufficient interest in the four-day game for it to be measured by more than membership numbers alone. There are also those members of the public who turn up to watch from time to time, when they have time, who read about it in the papers, or would if the papers gave it their full attention, or who follow it online. But he is concerned that any structure that diminishes four-day cricket as a competitive professional sport is not only retrograde but also downright dangerous.

'Once you've done that, you can't get it back,' he says, and there's no arguing with that. 'The quality of four-day cricket at the moment, in terms of its competitive parts, is such that we shouldn't give up investing in it. We should be talking it up and making it the most popular summer sport in England, not because we're suddenly going to get 10,000 or 15,000 people through the gates but because we can fuel an interest in the game generally that would have a beneficial impact on our revenues and, more than that, would create an atmosphere in which the rest of cricket would prosper.'

If ever an opportunity presented itself to talk up the entire county game, it was England's 3-1 Ashes victory in Australia in 2010-11. For a couple of weeks cricket was the good news on everyone's lips, taking minds off the coldest winter in memory and the bleakest economic forecasts in a generation. Was it really an interest in cricket, though, or just another burst of triumphalism occasioned by a rare victory on the old enemy's home turf? The feel-good factor that accompanied England's 2005 Ashes win had a genuine legacy in the surge of interest in recreational cricket, and as we've seen it was reward for the ECB's strategy of twinning Test success to grass-roots participation. The counties, who initially produce the Test-match heroes, deserve better than being piggy-in-the-middle between Team England and grass-roots England. They, too, should be sharing the legacy, not only in financial terms but in public awareness and audience participation.

Making the most of England's success, however, requires a proper marketing strategy for county cricket, a long-term strategy with, for example, well-researched and well-analysed data on the audience for cricket. Because investing in cricketers is not enough. If cricket is to have a future as a professional domestic game, there has to be investment in the audience as well. To bring in gate revenue, yes, but equally so that the television cameras at county matches have groups of spectators to focus on rather than panning away from the empty seats in search of the man and his dog. County cricket has to up its image; it needs to be marketed as an event people will want to attend. There is also the need for an audience to watch the game on television. Those able to watch these things tell me that cricket has been well served by Sky's coverage of domestic competitions, but even a multi-platform broadcaster like Sky wants audience numbers. Advertising income may not be the central plank of its business model right now, in the way subscribers are, but its ad revenue from cricket is worth in the region of £10 million a year. That's not small beer, and it's in cricket's interest as well as Sky's that those advertisers have an audience.

I don't know what the ECB's marketing budget is for Championship cricket. I suppose there is one, but given the shout they made about their million-pound marketing budget for Twenty20 in 2010, it can't be great. Not that the Twenty20 million was all spent on public-focused advertising and promotion; something like £600,000 went on 'dugouts and that sort of thing', I was told. That sounds to me more like a budget for the delivery of the event on behalf of the sponsor, than a flog-the-product marketing budget. They do the Campbell well at the ECB these days.

And let's face it, £1 million is scraps in national marketing terms. Talking about cricket with someone from a large plc marketing department, I attempted to put the game into context as a business by saying that Manchester United's wage bill was greater than the ECB's turnover. If that was the case, she laughed, her company's marketing budget was more than the ECB's turnover. Even so, small time or big time, cricket needs to be pumping out the message that there's a competitive first-class game that doesn't cost as much as Test matches, is available regularly (once someone sorts out the Steve Van Zandt fixture list) and is as integral to their country's life as to their community's. 'The counties are England and England is the counties,' Andy Nash said, which sounds rather like a take on something in *The Jungle Book*. The point is clear enough though: county cricket is there for everyone. Of course it would be a mighty help if the sales pitch could guarantee the presence of the game's big-name players. Cricket must be one of the few sports where you can't see your heroes playing in a domestic game, and that can't be a sound policy for its health 'going forward'. Getting the heroes down from the Team England pedestal and into their county grounds would be.

'Within the ECB strategic document they have a chapter called Vibrancy,' David Harker said, 'but it's not clear from the plan how we will encourage people to take an interest, to come along and watch. Because if you're at the ECB the primary focus tends to be Team England.'

With something like 65 non-playing staff associated with the England Cricket set-up, it probably is.

'Then there's political pressure to do stuff at the grass roots about recreational cricket, so the domestic game in all its guises often seems to come a poor third.'

'If this business were a brewery,' Stewart Regan observed, 'you'd know how many barrels you could produce and you'd have estimates of what your consumption rates were. You'd know who your consumer was, you'd know what it took to promote your product to that consumer and you'd have a budget to do it.'

I rather think the ECB has been leaving that side to the individual counties. So as Sussex are more successful than most clubs when it comes to domestic gate receipts, Dave Brooks seemed a good man to ask how they went about pulling punters off the street and into the ground. I wouldn't say Hove is always full, but they attract a good enough crowd to produce a nice atmosphere for watching cricket. And for playing it, I hope. 'We have a number of partnerships,' he explained. 'We try to get out into the pubs and the recreational clubs. That's a very simple method of communicating. There are 241 clubs in the county. Our partnership with Greene King gives us access to their pub network, so we can get fixture cards into pubs, use beer mats and all sorts of things to push the message. We've got, I suspect most counties have, contra arrangements with local newspapers and the local radio stations, who are pretty good at supporting cricket even if it's only commentary via the Internet. They're all happy to support the message of what's happening in local cricket. You can harness a lot of free media or contra media to push the game.

'Ultimately, though, you're marketing at the general public, which means a different consumer demographic between Twenty20 and Championship cricket. You could even say there's a different demographic between our Friday night Twenty20 and our Sunday afternoon Twenty20, because it's not necessarily the same group of people coming to those games. The Friday night beer fest is a very different marketing opportunity from the Sunday afternoon family-friendly occasion.'

Paul Millman recalled that when Twenty20 started, 'There was a lot of genuine hard-core research done on finding our potential audience. What we haven't done since is track the audience to see how the profile has changed and shifted. We don't really know enough now about who goes, and that's a great pity because you could target some advertising then.'

'That's an area where perhaps the ECB could lead,' Brooks said. 'They've got some very good CRM [customer relationship management] systems with information gathered around the World Twenty20 in 2009. Because most of us have pretty poor CRM systems, they could centralise the data collection.'

'And you could do it, albeit to a lesser extent, on Championship cricket,' Millman thought, 'or the 40-over competition now it's been revamped. You should be able to take a snapshot of who turns up and track their attendance. Then you can answer the question. I don't think it's fair to ask what the target market is without knowing what your current audience is, and it's not impossible to get that information. That should be a central role, and the sad thing is that the research seems to have lapsed. At Kent the members used to come round saying you must know who's attending and when we're attending. We had the systems but we didn't have a cat in hell's chance of digesting the data. It's there, and it's there probably to a lesser or greater extent by 18 counties.'

Maybe this provides a good example of an area where the counties would come into their own as a single division, having their own chief executive. Within that structure, they could work together on a single CRM platform and ticketing system. They could even go further and look at ways of combining back-office functions in the way that corporations do, for example by centralising the way they obtain sponsorships and advertising. These are essential areas of the business, and yet they're too often the first to suffer from cost cutting in hard times. The playing staff are usually sacrosanct.

It might even be a way of slimming down the ECB's 200-plus payroll. True, that figure includes cricketers (24 according to the 2009 accounts), umpires (26), coaching staff (46) and development staff (59), but it still leaves 60 in the admin bloc. No one I spoke to knew for sure what they all did, but isn't that always the way with bureaucracies? One county chief paraphrased the feelings of most when he said 'the mind boggles at the level of administrative cost within the ECB.' Indeed I'm sure there are county chairmen and chief execs, as they try to take non-cricket costs out of their own clubs (cutting back on staff to you and me), who view the ECB as the biggest cost base in English cricket. Reduce that and there'd be more money for all the stakeholders.

The most recent five-year draft plan, I was told, contained two big numbers that surprised my source. And while he wouldn't quote them for reasons of confidentiality, he fingered the cost of the England team, along with its back-up support, and the administration cost of the ECB. 'There are two elements within the ECB cost,' he went on. 'The part that supports professional cricket and the part that supports recreational cricket, and the part that seems most overblown is the part that supports recreational cricket.'

As for the Team England costs, the ECB accounts for 2009 reveal that £25.7 million was spent on all areas of international cricket, from players to coaches to management, tour costs and the National Performance Centre at Loughborough. That's a little over 70 per cent of what the 18 counties received.

As for discovering where all the money goes, trying to find answers in the ECB's annual accounts is like getting to grips with cosmology. Black holes immediately come to mind, or maybe that was something I picked up from someone else's mind.

'A friend of mine is a forensic accountant,' Rod Bransgrove said over an easy-drinking Françoise Chauvenet Chablis, 'and bear in mind that the ECB is audited by reputable firms, he says he doesn't know how they get away with it. What accounts don't say is always as important as what they do say, and this was illustrated not numerically but factually in the Annual Report for the year in which the Stanford debacle took place. Do you know that the whole wretched affair wasn't even mentioned in the Chairman's Report?'

I'm no accountant, forensic, chartered or turf, so don't take my back-of-a-postage-stamp numbers as fiducial. Think of them more as the factual side of fiction, or the other way round if you prefer. It's only money after all.

As Bransgrove drew to my attention some months after our summer Chablis, so saving me space on my postage stamp, 'in 2009 the ECB received total revenues of £114 million [£114,462,000 actually]. However, only £41 million [£40,770,015] of this permeated through to the stakeholders' – the stakeholders in this instance being the first-class counties, MCC, the Minor Counties Cricket Association, the minor counties and the county cricket boards. Don't think quality; just feel the width.

So we're left with £73,691,985. Wages, salaries and the associated costs such as pensions and National Insurance for the 215 aforementioned employees amounted to £18,178,000, which gets us down to £55,513,985. Charitable donations, mostly to the Cricket Foundation but excluding the ECB's contribution to its subsidiary, the England and Wales Cricket Trust Limited, were £4,905,000; rent to MCC was £223,395, insurance premiums were £1.4 million give or take, and just under a million went to such needy recipients as the Danish and Dutch cricket associations, the Irish and the Scots, a few privileged universities and the Professional Cricketers' Association. Which gets us down to a round £48 million to set aside for a rainy day. Or even a sunny one. The 2009 accounts reveal almost £20 million outstanding in loans made to the first-class counties and others, so some of that rainy-day 48 obviously goes into reserves. And then there's the tranche of various England Cricket costs, not forgetting travel and accommodation for the junket junkies and the wags with their beach bags, babies, buggies, nannies and grannies.

You can't blame the cash-strapped counties for casting covetous glances towards headquarters and wondering if they need that kind of governing body. Growing the 'state' at the expense of the market isn't quite what you think of as appropriate behaviour for a conservative sport like cricket. Messrs Cameron and Osborne might like to have a word in someone's ear next time the Lord's suits and blazers go to No. 10, what with localism and all that smaller government stuff being their *tote du jour*.

I didn't intend going down that road. For someone with an interest in how business works I have a reckless disinterest in money. To me it's like a batsman's runs and average. What interests me more is the way he goes about scoring them, the way he constructs his innings and the strokes he plays. So with business I'm fascinated more by company structures, management style and leadership qualities than I am by bottom lines and balance sheets. Like aggregates and averages they tell only part of the story. They're a shorthand or a ready reckoner for a quarter, a year, a season, a career. Meaning no disrespect to the number crunchers.

It's why the divisiveness in cricket took my attention when I began talking to people at the counties. Human nature being what it is, and Yorkshiremen being what they are, there's bound to be disagreement some of the time. But all of the time? That's a tad excessive even for a game not as gentlemanly as it's reputed to be – except when played by women.

'The whole problem with sport in this country,' Vinny Codrington told me early on, setting me up with background on the counties, 'is that it's club led rather than led at national level. You'll never get everybody to agree to something because they're all too parochial, all concerned with their own little interests. Tennis is a shining example of that, but then so is rugby and so is cricket. Unless we can get clear leadership, the county game is going to become more and more parochial and we'll get more and more entrenched, more dog eats dog, which is not equivalent to the game we're playing. I think we're heading for difficult times.'

That might account for many counties lamenting the absence of a master plan, a grand design that incorporates all 18 counties. I'm not aware there has been an audit of resources, for example, which addresses the needs of the game as a business in its entirety. The counties have been left to decide for themselves what they want to be, rather than having some lead from the top. There's management, no one disputes that, but little leadership, no vision.

'We certainly have not had a clear strategy for the venues and for first-class cricket,' Colin Povey agreed, and as we've seen the reality of that is encompassed in the conundrum of capacity versus demand, of too many big-match grounds and not enough matches. Should it have been a leadership issue, I suggested to Rod Bransgrove, reprising Paul's point earlier to Andy Nash. Should the ECB have said there were going to be only so many international grounds which would provide the major income? They would help develop those grounds and they'd divide the revenue among the counties as a dividend. But those promptings were me still trying to envisage the counties as a collective. All for one and one for all and all that. The disillusionment had yet to set in.

Bransgrove's response was to pour me another glass of wine – I wasn't driving – and argue that it wasn't necessarily the ECB's role to guide the counties. He probably knew I wouldn't find it easy to contradict the man who wasn't so much picking up the tab as owned the cellar. 'It is the counties, among others, remember that own the ECB, not vice versa. The fact that they may be imprudent or even inefficient *would*, in normal business circumstances, put them at the risk of failure. To some extent I thought what happened at Hampshire would have been a wake-up call for some counties but it wasn't. They just assume that someone or something will come along. It's for the counties to run their own businesses their own way and to ensure that they are receiving a proper distribution from central ECB income.'

I guess that's a no then.

Matthew Fleming thought that expecting the ECB to be responsible for the leadership as well as the administration of the counties was akin to expecting the impossible. 'I would say the ECB's role is to provide leadership in the administration of grass-roots and amateur cricket, which they do pretty well, and they're wired to administer Team England, which they also do fairly well. Relatively easy, some might say, but by and large they've got it right. I also think the administration of the professional game has been relatively efficient. The counties perceive much more management than they used to.'

Dave Brooks, having sat on an ECB working party, claims to have gone full circle several times when it comes to assessing the ECB's role in relation to the counties. 'When I joined Sussex I spent time trying to gauge how the governing body worked with us as a club. You go through a period of frustration at their lack of ability to deliver what the counties want, and then the longer you're involved you find yourself feeling sympathetic towards them. You realise the Board can't give the counties what they want because all the counties want something different. From the ECB's point of view, when you do consult with the 18 counties and you get 18 completely different replies, how on earth can you take account of those replies? So they end up saying, right, this is what we're going to do because the other options are no better or worse than what we've got.

'That then gets the counties asking what the point of the consultation was, because nothing's been changed. And the answer is that the counties as a group haven't given the Board any better options. So I kind of have some sympathy now. There's such disparity between the counties that it almost makes it impossible for the ECB to carry out a role through consensus, and that's why it gets so confusing. On the one hand you look to the ECB for leadership as the governing body. But on the other hand the governing body is owned by the counties, so the governance procedures within the ECB still require significant consultation, if not with the counties directly then through the committee structure. It doesn't really work and it almost can't work.

'If the ECB give leadership, the counties complain: "Why should the ECB tell us what to do? We're the chairmen, we own the ECB." Therefore all decision-making is painfully slow. And if the ECB don't give leadership we complain because no one's giving leadership, and we end up with random views from 18 counties, the MCC and anyone else who wants to add their two-penn'orth.'

And that, depressing as it is, pretty much sums up why no one has been driving county cricket forward in spite of there being, certainly from the outside looking in, a crying need for a helmsman rather than a steering group, a chorus-master instead of a choir. Matthew Fleming's analysis was that cricket was effectively a public company with shareholders – the counties and so forth – which is run like a private business, and certainly Brook's commentary brought to mind the kind of family business in which essential decisions are never taken because family members can never agree. They're the stuff of television drama. In real life the creditors usually break the impasse by sending in an outside chairman to knock heads together.

The difficulties, the contrariness, the contradictions and the failure to achieve consensus all reinforce the need for strong leadership, but instead this gets filed in the 'too difficult' or the 'wishful thinking' box. Neil Davidson, someone whose business acumen the game could have utilised more, was echoing others, chief executives maybe more than chairmen, when he said that the counties would continue to struggle 'until we get some proper leadership at the top'.

But what does that mean exactly? What does leadership entail for the counties in their relationship with the ECB? And if, as Andy Nash proposed, there is a vacuum within the ECB executive and an absence of strong leadership, shouldn't the county chairmen themselves, men like Nash, be the ones working for change?

'You're assuming we're not,' he answered. 'We've made very strong representations to the ECB about changes in the domestic structure, but we prefer to make those representations direct rather than shout our heads off through the media. There have been something like five Domestic Structure Reviews in the last three years, and out of those has come chaos. Vic Marks, who chairs our cricket committee, said that if we'd had a normal English spring in 2010 the Championship would have been a busted flush by the end of May. The whole thing would have been rain affected.

'So what should happen? People on six-figure salaries need to consult the counties, then having done that they need to do what they're paid to do. Take some decisions and get on and manage them.

'I can give you legion examples where the counties' best needs are not being met,' Nash went on, warming to his theme. 'Take the T20. The T20 is cricket's response to the decline in attendances. We've got to a situation now, we've been going since 2003, where Finals day is still a complete and utter shambles. What other sport would play two semi-finals, each game of which is much longer than a game of soccer, and longer still than a game of rugby union, and then a final. That's three games in the late summer here in England all in one day.

'You saw a complete farce, as we said it would be, at the Rose Bowl in 2010, with all three games rain affected. As a result the cricket was affected. I won't tell you what Murali Kartik said, but his grasp of Anglo-Saxon was surprisingly strong. What he meant was, how can you ask international-class cricketers to go out there and play on a wet pitch in the rain at night? Ludicrous! With ten overs to go the ground was emptying rapidly, and it was more than half empty by the time we got to the final ball.

'But the quarter-final! The T20 is, whether we like it or not, our FA Cup. Can you imagine a Premiership football club being told, "You're going to play your FA Cup quarter-final in the middle of the week and you're going to play it at an hour when most of your supporters are either at college or at work." We fought an enormous battle on that with the ECB and managed to get the starting time put back by 20 minutes! It's no good the ECB executive telling us the Sky contract says this and says that – they negotiated the Sky contract. Why didn't they have a list of mandatory requirements on behalf of the counties to make sure they made this an "FA Cup" that's fit for purpose?'

I'd guess the answer is that they weren't negotiating from a position of strength. No competitive bidder; no compulsion not to sell cricket for as much money as they could get their hands on; no compunction. Time perchance to segue into some Show of Hands, for old Gaunt is spent, his tongue a stringless instrument.

If the ECB cannot meet the needs of the counties, it is argued, there is reason for a new executive and a new structure. But how straightforward that would be is nowhere near as simple as saying there is a need for reform. These things take time and come in stages.

'A number of us think there's a strong argument for having a director or chief executive for domestic cricket,' David East said, and Jim Cumbes confirmed this. 'We need a champion, a representative of the chief executives who represents the domestic game to the Board. We're stuck in the middle between the England side of the business and the recreational game, and nobody seems to care about the domestic game other than the counties themselves. There's even a lack of understanding at the centre as to how cricket clubs operate.'

Somebody must have been listening, for at the end of 2010 the ECB promoted their head of venue partnerships, Gordon Hollins, to the new position of managing director – county business. His role, explained ECB chief executive David Collier, would 'encompass direct communication with all first-class counties, assisting and enhancing county business plans, facilities for members and supporters, and also ensuring benefit from the performance-related pay model.' Hold the horses. Where's any mention of the ubiquitous Domestic Structure Review and bringing some relief to the Mafeking of schedule congestion? Shouldn't that come within the county managing director's brief, or does the hierarchy think it's none of his 'county business'? I hope I'm not being too cynical, but there's a danger that Hollins's appointment comes with the hallmarks of a bureaucratic two-step, one forward, one back. An appointment to appease rather than take a cricketing and commercial view of what Colin Povey calls 'the opportunity space occupied by first-class cricket'. On the other hand he did think that Hollins had handled the venue partnership relationship with the counties well, so maybe there's hope.

Ideally, the counties' managing director should be heading up his own operating board and looking after every element of county cricket. However, like England's Ashes success in Australia, Hollins's appointment has introduced an opportunity to focus attention on the counties. His ECB equivalent Hugh Morris, in his role as managing director – England Cricket, has shown what can be accomplished through intelligent leadership, proper investment and attention to detail. It would be the right step forward for county cricket if Hollins were allowed to put in place a strategy for the domestic game which mirrors that which proved so effective for England's international game.

It's time, for example, to get the county game back in the national newspapers. There's more to English cricket than Test matches and international players being rolled out in rotation to feed journalists with a daily diet of dressing-room jargon and platitudes. I know there's the Internet, and everyone with a mobile phone has access to scores and blogs, Test teamsters' tweets and every other fascinating irrelevance of the microchip media, but you don't glance over someone's shoulder to read a match report on their BlackBerry. It's just not done. I understand, too, that there'll come a time when a state education is no guarantee of the ability to read, but we haven't got there yet.

As I mentioned at the start, rugby union club coverage has been outgunning county club cricket by something like four to one in column inches. By way of a defence the papers say that county cricket has a product problem, and to some extent that's true. There are too many forms of the game to provide a cohesive narrative across a season. But that was also the case 30 to 40 years ago when county cricket staged four competitions and still outperformed club rugby in space and the quality of the coverage.

The Woodcocks and Arlotts, the Streetons, Melfords and the Swanton were able to craft essays on Championship cricket at Lord's and Basingstoke, Chesterfield, Cheltenham and Canterbury, while Alan Gibson regaled his own purring, devoted readers on the delights and perils of changing trains and buying buns at Didcot when en route to Oxford for a university game. A university game! County cricket was a literary event back then, and men like Colin Dredge, the Sunday League's Demon of Frome, danced in Times roman before the eyes of Monday morning commuters as they waited for their trains at Clapham Junction. Cricket took its eye off the ball and dropped the catch; rugby union spotted the gap and went for it like an old-time England centre. It won't be easy to make up the lost ground, but if county cricket is to emerge from the consciousness backwater it's been drifting along, the game has to be marketed, and marketed hard. That is a top-down job; it has to be part of a strategy that everyone buys into.

From the conversations Paul and I had, and allowing for the fact that people were speaking their minds in a way not generally encouraged at ECB meetings, I did wonder how much the perceived lack of leadership was more a reflection of the management style of the senior officers at the ECB. Certainly the message I was getting was of management that exercised strong, tight control over all aspects of the business, that wanted to be both drummer and dancer. That kind of management isn't necessarily a weakness, but it does require a process of checks and balances that allows directors, stakeholders and even those lower down the administrative ladder to say, 'Whoa, stop for a moment, where are we going with this, why are we doing it?' What it doesn't need is a supine board of directors that turns turtle, has its tummy rubbed and rubber stamps whatever the executive presents it with. Maybe the ECB isn't like that, but out in the shires that is one perception.

CHAPTER FIFTEEN
TIME FOR A
'C' CHANGE

For reasons best understood by themselves, a large swathe of Americans are convinced that their 44th president, Barack Obama, is a socialist. In which case don't say this too loudly next time you attend a stateside tea party, but American football has been rooted in a socialist system from 1935, when the reverse-order draft for players was introduced as a means of levelling the playing field. Since then the NFL has added to its left-wing credentials by sharing equally among its clubs the revenue earned from television rights and other centralised income streams. 'While the NFL's collectivist bent might bother some fans in what is arguably still the most capitalist country on the planet,' Mark Yost writes in *Tailgating, Sacks, and Salary Caps*, 'it's hard to argue with its success.'

That success can be measured not only by economic qualifiers such as attendances, merchandising, television viewing figures, ad rates and the like. It can also be measured out on the gridiron where clubs big and small compete on more or less equal terms. Whereas if you look at many sports in Britain, they try to create inequality rather than equality. You need look no further than football's Premier League to observe that, with the same few teams hogging the high life year after year.

'The whole philosophy of American sports,' noted Mark Newton, 'and so too in English cricket, is to create balance. One of the ways of doing that is to have equal distribution of money. For me that's the critical factor in creating balance of competition. We don't know which counties are going to be in the top three or four each season, we can only guess, and that keeps our sport interesting.'

But it's not only on the field of dreams that balance is so important. As Yost quotes the owner of the New England Patriots, 'We compete against each other three hours a week. Otherwise, we have aligned interests.' The clubs' owners acknowledge that by acting together they make more money than by going it alone. If only cricket's county chairmen and chief executives were to take that line. The chasm that's been growing between the Category A and Category C grounds is but one example of vested interests prevailing.

Funnily enough chasm didn't feature in the C list that Paul Millman scribbled down towards the end of our interviews and conversations. Topping the bill were conflict and cooperation, followed in no significant order by consumer, communication, cohesion, coordination, continuity, community and, finally, cricket's crossroads.

Surrey's Paul Sheldon came up with another when we began discussing what it would take to coordinate the disparate business models around the counties, to persuade them to achieve cohesion and cooperation. 'You'll never get a consensus,' he said, to which Paul Millman responded, 'Well then, is that the issue?'

Neil Davidson would agree it is, and we know he keeps two other Cs in his locker, constitution and cooperative. A career in the dairy business has obviously made him familiar with the ways of cooperatives and trade associations, so it is not unexpected to hear him say that English cricket has much in common with a trade association. It's worth noting also that David East, another to refer to the counties as a collective, was in the wine trade, with its many cooperative businesses, before his return to Essex. Like Yost with regard to the NFL, I've long thought of English cricket as being based on socialist or collectivist principles while administered in the main by Conservatives, capitalists and free-market Liberals. The international branch of the business produces the bulk of the game's revenue via television rights and so forth, and this is then distributed down the line. If it works for cricket, who's to say it shouldn't work for a whole society? Other than the Tea Party poopers, that is.

Having come from a farming country, I empathised with Davidson when he spoke of English cricket being best served by the cooperative model. The New Zealand cooperative, Fontera, is owned by some 11,000 dairy farmers, whose interests are served by a board of 13 directors and an executive committee, and represented by a national sharehold-ers' council. You'd think if 11,000 Kiwi farmers from different rugby provinces can pool their differences as well as their milk, it wouldn't be such a big deal for 18 county chairmen, regardless of personality, ego or pure native bloody-mindedness, to manage something similar. But apparently it's not so straightforward. Like league football in the days before oil sheikhs, oligarchs and Americans – although it is still so in the lower divisions – county cricket has tended to attract its chair-men from a private business background, as often as not entrepreneurs whose management style as executive chairmen of their companies is to say this is how it's done. And if you want to keep your job, or your cushy seat on the board, that's usually how it gets done, right or wrong. It might explain why, when a few of them get together to work out a strategy for English cricket, their achievement rate doesn't always stack up against their other business achievements. Their cricket meetings are probably higher on testosterone than resolution.

An obstacle confronting the cooperative concept in England is that the word too frequently carries left-wing, working-class or Continental European connotations. For too many people, I suspect, the thinking is that cooperative is not one of us, as Margaret Thatcher might almost have said. But then her father only sold dairy products at the end of the milk chain. He made the final mark-up and pock-eted the profit. He didn't do the dairy bit two times a day, 365 days a year, the way that my grandparents, my aunts and Phil Archer did. So I had some idea what Davidson was talking about when he began by saying that, 'In the world of agriculture you have a lot of people with individual businesses who are members of a farmers' co-op. And in the cooperatives and trade associations I'm familiar with, you can only work on the basis of consensus.

'Consensus is hard work. It means the people who are leading the individual businesses, the counties, having to sit around the table and keep talking. There will be points of competition, but there is also a commonality there and if you actually work hard at it, you get a consensus. I went through the milk industry in the 1990s when we saw the end of the milk-marketing scheme and there was a lot of competition between the dairy companies. But there was a lot of commonality as well, and we had to thrash out common positions to take in our dealings with the government and with the outside world. While remaining fierce competitors in the marketplace, it was in all of our interests to work together and be an effective trade association.

'Getting there,' he explained, 'required a major commitment from the principals of each major company, along with effective chairmanship supported by an efficient secretariat. During key periods the principals met on a monthly basis for a strict two hours to hammer out consensual strategies, and eventually we achieved the industry objectives. We did things like rotate the chairmanship so that nobody was chairman – they called it president – for more than two years, and later we employed an independent chairman purely because the commitment required by the role was too much for someone also running a major business.'

At a time when the counties are coming under external pressure as the IPL and ICC encroach on their domestic season and their players, and from internal pressure brought on by debt, the big-match bidding process and fixture congestion, the cooperative model could be not merely desirable but vital if English professional cricket is to ride out the perfect storm brewing up around it. Achieving this model, however, will require a quantum leap of Lillee-like dimensions in the way the counties regard themselves and the cricket business. For a start they'd have to recognise that they are a cooperative and not a one-off operation in competition with 17 others both on and off the field.

'You'd have to have all 18 chairmen around a table and you thrash out a model,' Davidson continued.

Just as the NFL did in 1935, in fact.

'If it takes 12 months to thrash out the model, then fine, let it take 12 months provided there's a commitment to mature debate and consensual decision-making. However,' he warned, 'that needs a very good chairman with a skills set who is strong enough on the one hand to lead the model forward and at the same time doesn't want to dominate and put his own stamp on it. He has to try to get consensus, to get the county chairmen to buy into the cooperative model.'

In other words, to do what's best for county cricket as opposed to what's best for themselves and their own county. It's asking a lot, and the irony hasn't escaped me that when push came to shove at Leicestershire in 2010, chief executive David Smith and chairman Davidson were unable to reconcile their differences. That the falling-out was primed by the county's poor on-field performances provides a suitable illustration, were one needed, of how volatile the relationship is between business and sport. When conciliation, cooperation, cohesion and however many other positive Cs are called for, all too often sadly it's the negative Cs such as conflict and combativeness that come out of their corner the stronger. It's the age-old story: putting theory into practice is a lot harder than devising the theory in the first place. Which is no reason not to keep on trying, and why I'm not sidelining the cooperative concept just yet.

But let's look at another C that's not on Paul's list: chairman. Has the ECB yet had a chairman who possessed the inclination, the patience or even the ambition to drive forward a cooperative model for the counties? There have been only three. Ian MacLaurin was, by reputation, a corporate chairman par excellence who, on the few occasions I talked to him at length, struck me as frustrated by the counties' inability to pull together for the greater good of the game. David Morgan's background was with British Steel, and all the bureaucratic baggage that a state-owned business carries with it. The strength there, I suspect, was conciliation, for without it nothing would get done. The current chairman, Giles Clarke, is an entrepreneur. All had their critics, Clarke perhaps more so, but what chairman doesn't, whether in commerce or sport? He is said to be confrontational (another C word) on the one hand, and on the other someone who makes decisions according to what he believes is best for cricket. One county chief executive said that, 'Love him or hate him, in Giles Clarke we're probably as close as we've ever been in having a strong chairman.' Others suggest he was fortunate to survive the ECB's involvement with the Stanford millions and their handling of English clubs' participation in the Champions League.

If I have a criticism of Clarke as chairman it's that he comes out of the counties and was voted in by the counties, as indeed Morgan was before him. There is a strong case for saying the time has come for the ECB to have an independent, paid chairman. There's certainly a momentum gathering behind that idea, with support, I gather, in government circles. The way the chairmanship is now, there is always the possibility of a chairman having a vested interest in his own county and also in maintaining the support of those counties that voted for him. The role is too important to be a political one, with deals being done in smoke-free rooms and hospitality suites.

Indeed, if the counties are not to lurch from crisis to crisis, as some believe they are, the ECB do need governance that is transparent and projects a clear, long-term view of the business as a whole; that can get the best out of the staff by delegating effectively and by encouraging people to realise their true potential.

History tells us that the organisations and societies that thrive best are those in control of their own destinies. My intuition tells me that English cricket's domestic destiny, as perceived by the ECB, does not stretch beyond a string of strategy documents ring-fenced by short-term television agreements. That does not really constitute controlling one's destiny; and a New Zealand cynic might add that English cricket's destiny is in the hands of a natural-born Australian media mogul. To paraphrase some business speak – it's catching – I'd go so far as to wonder if centrally there is a holistic overview of UK Cricket plc. For as Neil Davidson put it when we were discussing cooperatives, 'There should have been a proper blueprint for the game, setting out what we are trying to achieve – a pyramid system that's developing an England cricket team which maximises revenues that then flow back down through the counties and through the recreational game so that the system keeps perpetuating itself. Instead it's still all about self-interest.'

If you were to draw up such a blueprint, be it for a cooperative or whatever, one of the first questions asked would have to be, 'What is the ECB for?' You don't hear it being asked very often. Is it for the recreational game, is it for the England teams, is it for the counties? Is it to bring in as much money as it possibly can, irrespective of where that money comes from?

'There are all sorts of different questions,' a county executive said over lunch, 'and it's time there was a proper debate around them. One thing you might question is whether the remit of the ECB is far too wide. There could be a much smarter way of structuring the game, with maybe the MCC taking a bigger role.'

I put that point to Matthew Fleming, the MCC man on the ECB board of directors. 'Although the MCC lost its traditional position in the game's administration some years ago,' he said, 'it didn't lose its desire to have a focus. If, for instance, the current structure of the ECB were to be reviewed and streamlined some time in the future, I'd be surprised if the MCC, which doesn't receive any money from the ECB, wasn't approached to do again some of the things it used to do so the ECB can get on with running the professional game.

'The MCC has quietly gone about doing what it can in world cricket. And quietly the MCC's brand has either gone up because others' brands have fallen, or it's a combination of others falling and MCC doing some very good things. I think it's probably the latter. As such, I suspect, MCC would have a sense of responsibility to consider how it could share the load. We sponsored the Spirit of Cricket Test matches [between Australia and Pakistan in England in 2010] because we think that is part of MCC's wider role in cricket, and at the moment we pay for university cricket. I'm sure the more enlightened MCC members and even some of the diehards understand that the club's wider role might in time involve helping with an element of the amateur game.'

Neil Davidson agrees. 'They're an organisation without a role. I would give the recreational game to the MCC, within the framework of the ECB. I'd say to them, you need a role in the game and English cricket needs a proper development system. You've got a lot of money, a lot of resources, a lot of brains within the club. Get stuck in and organise the recreational game rather than getting involved in franchises.'

There are potential sticking-points for this suggested role, however. One is what initially contributed to the club losing its power base in English cricket. Is a private members' club the proper conduit for government money? Cricket currently receives something like £38 million from Sport England and, David East reminded me, Sport England and the government want to see a governance structure for cricket that supports the whole game. MCC working within the framework of the ECB is unlikely to be contentious but if, as has been floated, the ECB were to be split into international and domestic divisions, this arrangement might fail to meet Sport England's 'whole sport' concept. It shouldn't. It's not as if the two divisions would be entirely stand-alone businesses. They would come under the umbrella of a much slimmed-down ECB governance, that's all, and MCC's role would be within that context.

But within which division, because a third would merely be additional bureaucracy? Maybe it wouldn't have to be either division. I'm sure there's nothing to prevent head-office ECB receiving the government funding, as it does now, and then contracting out responsibility for the recreational game to the MCC. In as much as one is ever expected to understand government policies, isn't this what the Westminster coalition (another C) set out as a model for, say, education and health?

The point of the exercise has to be effectiveness and simplicity, not complexity. But I don't see the counties buying it. Many of them have close ties with their county cricket boards and, in spite of the added financial burden should ECB funding be cut back, those counties would be reluctant to relinquish that relationship. There could also be an unintended consequence.

'If the county boards reported elsewhere,' Andy Nash said, seeing where I was going before I'd even got there, 'what would probably happen is the professional counties grabbing control of the age-group players in the way the soccer clubs have. That would debilitate the county boards and leave them looking after the adult amateur game and schools cricket minus the cream of the talent.'

That's the trouble with ideas: they're rather like physics. Where there's a positive there's also a negative. Not that it stops people having them.

'Why do we have only 18 counties so called first-class?' Mark Newton asked, a question that had crossed my own mind countless times. 'We actually have 38 counties, and my view is that all 38 counties should be in a proper pyramid.'

Mine too, if I remember correctly what I once wrote in *Wisden* about the fallibility of a structure that resembles a series of housing projects linked horizontally by inhospitable walkways rather than the pyramidal staircase that works for football and, as we've seen, for rugby. In which case, why not push the divisional structure even further and extend Sport England's 'whole sport' concept to a visionary dimension as far as cricket is concerned?

Nothing would please Newton more, he said, 'if Cornwall, for instance, found themselves a benefactor who decided to build Cornwall up as a cricket side, knowing he could emulate Durham and go all the way to the top. That would be great for cricket, in the way that the rise of Worcester and more recently Exeter was great for rugby. It would be a sign of vision and strategy from the ECB.'

Paul and I began putting the pyramid idea around, receiving a varied but not always negative set of reactions. David Smith thought that supporting 18 counties was challenging enough for a game that was already creaking financially. Nor was he persuaded by the argument that the minor counties already received ECB funding as stakeholders in the current structure and would not necessarily receive more unless they climbed the staircase. There could still be, for argument's sake, 18 fully professional clubs in the top two leagues of the pyramid, followed by a semi-professional third league and below that the remainder of the counties distributed in the most appropriate construct, be it more leagues or regional divisions. The potential for movement was the essence of the model, and promotion would not have to be mandatory or an automatic right. There could be play-offs but counties would first have to meet certain conditions, such as statutory facilities, before they could go up. And while we're at it, how about a 38-county Twenty20 knockout to give the format a truly national focus?

'It's an interesting concept,' Smith replied, 'but my gut tells me that 18 is where we are, the constitution supports 18, and I think that's where we'll stay. Because of the way our game is financed, I don't think you'd have many voting in favour of more. In effect, people would view more as meaning less for them.'

Ah, the old sweet song of self-interest. Andy Nash was more receptive. Something of a Darwinian when it comes to counties surviving or falling by the wayside – survival of the fittest and all that – he accepted that he had to respect the argument that other counties should be allowed their time in the sun if they were strong enough to get there. 'I'm not sure I'd go with promotion-demotion every season,' he said, 'but if you were to find yourself at the bottom of a division for, let's say, three years running, then I think yes, the game's up.'

Angus Porter's view, when he first took up his post as chief executive of the Professional Cricketers' Association, was that there were too many first-class counties. Funny how that strikes you as obvious when you come into cricket from the outside world. But, he agrees, he's not so sure of that now. 'I'm less certain because I don't think any of us properly understands the extent to which the international game in the UK, and the support for cricket in the UK, is sustained by the local demand that is nourished by the counties. Given that 90 per cent of the game's revenue and the Sky contract is all about the appetite for the international game, the relationship between the counties and England is something that has to be thought about quite deeply before we come to a conclusion about the right number of counties and the right structure.

'What is odd is that, with the recent exception of Durham, there are 18 counties for reasons of history, and it's not obvious to me why there should be 18 geographies in the country that have this unique position. I've lived for the last 25 years in Buckinghamshire, and club cricket, minor counties cricket, is very strong in Bucks. So the question I would ask is whether there is any less love for cricket in a minor county than there is in one of the first-class counties? I'm not certain there is.'

Porter agrees, nonetheless, that you wouldn't have 18 fully professional clubs to feed the national side if you were designing the English game from scratch. You'd certainly aim to eliminate the divide that exists between the first-class counties, currently receiving on average £1.8 million annually from the ECB, and the have-nots who don't get anything approaching that.

'You might start,' Porter said, 'by designing something that had six or eight regions that play cricket much more akin to the state structure in Australia, because one has obviously tended to see the Australian model as successful. Then you'd have to think what the level below that might look like. It might look like something that didn't sustain a full complement of professional players.'

As mentioned already, cricket is complicated more than some team sports by the different formats played. One-day games would be more suitable for competitions below the professional leagues simply because the three- and four-day game occupies so much time. And this time factor, Porter points out, makes it 'much less easy to be a semi-professional cricketer than it is to be a semi-professional footballer or rugby player. I've always thought that a side like Buckinghamshire, playing minor counties cricket, is drawing on a smaller pool of talent than it could, simply because it's drawing on those people who can afford the time to play the matches.'

Lots to think about then before any shake-up, which is the way it should be. As they say, there has to come a time for the talking to stop, but what's less often said is that there also has to be a time for the talking to start. I have a suspicion that for some counties, especially the Test match grounds, that time has already passed. If our conversations with the counties reinforced any preconceptions it was that, while everyone has different ideas, no one says the structure should remain the same. Change is in the air; what's unknown is the catalyst that will bring it about. It could be the IPL as more and more county players look to its greasy pole and put themselves up for auction, hoping Mr Green finds his way inside their garter. It could be that the big-match grounds finally take the bit between their teeth, break out on their own and turn the franchise fantasy into fact.

It could be some factor outside cricket altogether. No one has the foggiest notion what's going to happen to any economy in the next five years, be it cricket's, Britain's, Europe's or the world's, let alone the next ten. Politicians have made much talk about austerity, but as Matthew Fleming said all too pertinently, 'No one knows what austerity is in this current generation.' So maybe it's time for cricket to get the professionals in and do a brains-up, as the business-school boys like to say. If so, the outcome has to be answers and not just more analysis. We've been down that road and still find ourselves at a crossroads. It might even be the same crossroads we were at before.

After the publication of my 1993 book *Betrayal: The Struggle for Cricket's Soul*, a reviewer wrote that I'd presented enough of cricket's problems but provided no answers. I don't think I intended to. That book was written as a homage to Gibbon: it used the past to warn of what could happen in the future. This book is about the present. It sets out options for the future, something to stimulate discussion, but it was never intended to provide answers. Its stories are those that the people running the business of county cricket have to tell, and if there are answers the counties have first to agree on the problems. The only Cs they seem to have in common are cricket, counties, Championship and some kind of change.

CHAPTER SIXTEEN
FROM AGE TO AGE

From the St Helen's ground press box I'd sometimes look beyond the cricket to the white horses running over Swansea Bay. I was born in sight of the sea and until coming to London had never lived so far from it. The first glimpse of gulls gathering ahead of storm clouds still makes me nostalgic for it. At Swansea the clouds gathering across the bay meant rain as often as not and, if the umpires were in a decisive mood, an early end to the day's cricket. It might even mean a journey back as far as Bristol with David Foot for company, instead of Bruce Springsteen and Van Morrison. A different kind of story-teller; a poetic writer whose passion for sport and words was matched by his love of people and his belief in fair play in all walks of life. In better times we call it justice. Ragtop up or ragtop down you couldn't ask for a better travelling companion.

You could say David personified all that's worthwhile about county cricket, from his appreciation of talent and honest toil on the field to his pleasure in the presence of those around him on the other side of the boundary – and cricket lovers did gather around him. The acquaintances he'd built up down the years were legend. You'd see him standing among them anywhere in England but especially in the West Country, pint in hand, making good conversation and listening attentively, patiently, to anyone with a reminiscence or an opinion. And there are others like him, for that's where much of the enjoyment in county cricket lies. It's in the people watching and talking as much as in the cricketers batting, bowling and fielding. Maybe that's why Twenty20 supposedly appeals to a younger audience. The young have still to master the art of conversation. Mainlining the noise saves them having to think. Contrary to some opinions, the racket doesn't necessarily keep older spectators and county members away from Twenty20 games. They can plug their ears with cotton wool and, same as always, get on with the crossword in the *Daily Telegraph*.

But here's an interesting thought about county members. They don't all read the *Telegraph* these days, not for the cricket anyway. When Jim Cumbes was playing football his teammates would say to him, 'What are you doing with the bloody *Telegraph*? Are you a posh bugger?' The reason he read it was because it reported every county match. 'I was very loyal to the paper because they were loyal to county cricket,' he said, 'but now you're lucky to get a column, and if you get the column there might be three matches in the column.'

Now the members go online to the different websites, and not just for the scores, reports and team news. They also log on to county websites to let their chairman, their committee and their executive officers know exactly what they think about the current state of affairs, on and off the field. Rotten most of the time, if you're wondering. Kent's powers-that-be became so irritated by the constant carping that they closed down the county chat room. No probs, said the disgruntled of Tonbridge and Tunbridge Wells, we'll set up our own site, and they did. Pesky thing, the Internet. It's worse than having an AGM every day of the week.

It's not surprising, then, that some counties have begun saying aloud what many have been thinking for a long time. Members clubs, with their committees and sub-committees, are not the most relevant structure for a 21st century sporting business. 'We have probably the most old-fashioned governing structure there is,' one club told me. A frequently heard complaint is that the decision-making process slows down every time a significant issue has to go to the members for a vote. That's why governments insist on parliamentary democracy, and usually pay no more than lip service to referendums; it's why county clubs will try to slip through reforms and modernisation without first consulting the membership – until a few gimlet-eyed members get wind of it and wind up the blogosphere. It's one of the frustrations of county management that while members are not exactly shareholders in the business, in many ways they can and do exercise the rights of shareholders. For a start they vote in the chairman and the committee, which can give them disproportionate influence over the way a county operates. No wonder there are days when county clubs look downright dysfunctional.

Not that everyone opposes the membership structure. 'I think we are very privileged still to be a members' organisation in the 21st century,' said Somerset chairman Andy Nash. 'One of our great strengths is the healthy membership and its seven area committees.'

Even so, Somerset and other counties have streamlined their operations to stop the lunatic fringe trying to hijack their clubs, or steer them in a different direction. Moreover, Somerset are fortunate in not being held hostage by banks and other lenders. Not all the counties are this fortunate, as we know, and if borrowing becomes more difficult it will be interesting to note how lenders in future regard the security of loans to organisations whose chairmen are elected by people concerned mostly with what happens on the field; who would rather see £10,000 going towards a star player's salary than to reducing an overdraft or paying interest on a loan.

County members sitting in deckchairs or in front of the pavilion with their thermos flasks and sandwiches have been a cricket cliché for about as long as I can remember. They are, admittedly, of a certain age, or even older, and invariably they are described as a dying breed. As dying breeds go they are damned resilient – something to do with what they put in those thermos flasks maybe. They are, I guess, the modern equivalent of the leisured classes of the Victorian and Edwardian ages, except that they don't all have too much money to spend. They're not the add-on income stream beloved of treasurers and catering managers.

What they do have is time, and following Championship cricket does occupy time. Many of those going to games today have, by and large, retired from work and from raising children; the men, many of them anyway, have stopped playing club cricket, which along with work may be what kept them from watching county cricket in their younger days. Perhaps they are a continuation of the cliché, but they nonetheless remain cricketers at heart. Not so much old buffers as old batsmen and bowlers with memories of their own summer days and Sunday afternoons at the crease. There are generations behind them still, going in to bat and coming in to bowl, running slower every year from mid-on to mid-off, and one day some of them will want to gaze across the outfield at Chelmsford, Canterbury, Hove, Taunton, Northampton or Headingley and bemoan the paucity of talent in the modern game and their county's lowly ranking.

There could be more of them, too, if cricket's marketing men got their wits about them. With people living longer, we're told, and employment being squeezed, the retired and the pensioned-off are a growing demographic that the game should be tapping into. Where are the commercials for county cricket on afternoon telly? Look around and you see that more and more grandparents have become the family childminders, so where better to take a grandchild on a summer's day than the county ground. It's safe and there's room to run around. What better way to introduce a child to watching cricket? But it's not all one-way traffic. The counties need to ensure that there's enough to sustain the child's interest. I imagine today's girl and boy will expect a day at the cricket to mean a good deal more than watching cricket while granddad or grandma does the cross-word. Some more inclusiveness would help. Being on the Groucho wing of the Marxist persuasion, nothing put me more off county cricket than those boards on rope pronouncing 'Members only', with stewards in white coats manning the portcullis.

The members, you may recall, were the stymie – they might have been the bogey as well – when I proposed to Stewart Regan that counties should open their gates for Championship games, partly to provide spectators but more specifically to entice people to watch cricket. After all, the English can't resist a bargain. However, I was told by Regan and others, the members would baulk at paying subscriptions when their favourite format, the first-class game, was free of charge. And membership revenue, whatever size its contribution to turnover, is not something the clubs can afford to deny themselves. Even so, I suspect the time will come, if it hasn't already at some counties, when members have to acknowledge that their influence is on the wane.

In the meantime they can remain a thorn in the side of chairmen and chief executives who must meet as best possible their members' aspirations for a better season than last, or – much harder to do – manage an expectation of success, an entitlement to it even, that has been fed by the stories of past triumphs handed down from generation to generation.

'That's what the commercial world of sport is all about,' Mark Newton said. 'Managing expectations. To me the essence of watching sport is simple. If you go to watch your team's superstars and they fail to match your expectations, you go home disappointed. If your team is full of youngsters and they match your lower expectations of them, or perform better than your expectations, you go home happy.'

His philosophy was made manifest by his own county in 2010 when, having had their cricket budget slashed, Worcestershire gained promotion to Division One. 'The season before, 2009, we spent over a million on cricket for the first time on highly paid international-quality players, and it went wrong,' he explained. 'We didn't win a game in the Championship and were relegated. So we learnt from that. We were not prepared to put up with the egos and the negative influences in the dressing room, even if it meant six months of nightmare media coverage.' Not forgetting an end-of-season members' forum of former Yorkshire AGM proportions. 'Some of the players wanted to go. There were others to whom we said, "We're not paying you the same sort of money for not performing." Straightaway we cut £500,000 in salaries and we reinvested £200,000 of that in youngsters.'

Investing in youngsters is something close to Jamie Clifford's heart. The Kent chief exec had originally been the director of cricket development at the Kent Cricket Board. Prior to that, incidentally, he had worked for *Wisden*'s online operation. 'I'm sure I was very boring when I was running the cricket board,' he laughed. 'I was forever saying that we were producing all these young players and their progress was being blocked by the number of overseas players that Kent had at the time. But it was a sign of that particular time. The number of overseas players has now dropped.'

Kent supporters may like to know that around the country there are many just as incensed as they are that Rob Key's progress as an England cricketer was equally blocked by 'overseas' players. 'Maybe he'd be one of those who isn't quite good enough,' I heard a former player say, 'but we'll never know unless we play him enough.'

But back to Jamie Clifford and managing expectations. 'It was important that we sat down and set out our guiding principles and our level of expectations. For one thing, it immediately affects player recruitment. Take 2011, for example. We were relegated in the Championship in 2010, so was it realistic to think we could bounce back into Division One straightaway? Given our financial resources, possibly not. So we set out to be competitive in the one-day competitions, to get to the knockout stages, and to finish in the top half of Division Two. That seemed to be a realistic ambition.

'I do know, though, that our players will give everything to win every game. We're bringing in home-grown players, and there's been excitement among the members at that prospect. Also excitement at the fact that it's still possible to have a county club that can rely on their own development system to produce their next generation of cricketers, of Kent cricketers. If at the same time this brings player salaries to a manageable level and helps bring the business back into kilter, then we win on both fronts.'

Now that the ECB are using performance-related fee payments to encourage counties to play more under-22s and under-26s, the chances are that county cricket will become a youngster's game anyway. The days of the gnarled old pro hanging on for an extra year may well be numbered. This should not mean, however, that he and his kind are lost to the game. Research by Neil Davidson, not so many years ago, revealed a sizeable number of England-qualified county cricketers aged over 28 who were never likely to play international cricket. There will be one or two like Chris Tremlett whose hour in the sun is at hand, but his talent had long been logged and ledgered. It was simply taking longer to reach fruition, and he needed more time in county cricket to achieve it. There are others, though, for whom the word journeyman was coined.

'That group,' said Davidson, 'should be coming out of county cricket earlier and going back into club cricket to make that standard better. We must all the time be trying to raise the standard of our club cricket. So instead of these players standing around eking out another year's contract, holding back the talented youngsters we're identifying as having the ability to be county cricketers, we want them to spend the next 10 to 20 years being bloody good club cricketers.'

Age concern is something the PCA is conscious of, Angus Porter said. 'We define our role as safeguarding the interest of cricketers past, present and future, and as an organisation we're devoting an increasing proportion of our time to thinking about the future. The longer you play county cricket, the more difficult it is to have a successful career post-cricket. It's much easier to retrain or begin a different career when you're in your mid-20s than it is in your mid-30s. The most important thing we can do in that respect is have education programmes and help people to get work placements and so forth.

'The people I feel most responsible for are those who have to move on to a life after cricket before they're prepared for that move. As an association, we've got to get to a position where they're getting into good habits right from the start of their career in terms of thinking about personal development.'

Paradoxically, the PCA's view as a players' union is that an age-based quota policy should not be countenanced if it discourages the selection of the strongest side. Similarly, in the debate about the fixture programme and the sustainability of the county game, the PCA's vote has traditionally been influenced by its desire to maximise the number of current members it can keep in full-time employment on a county contract. It's just another example of the conflicts and contradictions swirling around county cricket.

Yet at the same time there is a lot more to the PCA's position than ensuring new contracts. The players, like the county members, regard the County Championship as paramount and would be reluctant to consider changes to the domestic structure which might compromise its integrity. As well as being the competition they all want to win, the Championship is the pathway to the fulfilment of every cricketer's dream and ambition – to play Test cricket for his country. As Test cricket's criterion should be quality and not quantity, there's much good sense in the players and their association arguing that the current hectic playing schedule is not conducive to cricket of the highest quality, or for that matter to preparing players for international cricket.

Heaven alone knows how you come up with a structure that suits everyone once you start taking in the cricketers, the chairmen and committees that employ them, television, the commercial men and the members. Few of the interested parties view the game through a wide-angle lens; they prefer to use a telephoto, magnifying what they want to see through a narrow field of vision. That's not a criticism, more a reflection on the human condition, and it won't take the threat of a crisis to change that. It will take the crisis itself.

Will there be one? Is the county game really in crisis, or merely in a mess of its own making? What isn't these days? It does need reform, maybe even something radical, and has done for a long time. Just about everyone agrees on that. What the previous pages have shown is that they can't much agree on anything else. If they could sort out that problem and manage some consensus, they may get closer to resolving the more difficult challenges.

During the months I was visiting the counties there was a lot of media talk about unsustainable levels of debt and of counties going bust. This should be kept in proportion. Most businesses are built on borrowing. I once suggested that a company I was consulting should carry a year's profit forward with a view to reducing its subsequent borrowing requirements. I saw it as a process of converting interest payments into dividends 'going forward'. The shareholders at the meeting looked at me as if I was mad. The annual profit was already committed to school fees and paying for the ski chalet in Switzerland. Besides, the finance guy pointed out, the interest was tax deductible. Why would you want to do away with it?

Cricket is not really a big business – think Manchester United's wage bill – and, as one or two people expressed it, unlike football it would take an extraordinary combination of circumstances to send a county to the wall. In Angus Porter's opinion, 'The sums of money involved, certainly to keep the smaller counties afloat, are not so great that it's impossible to find a sugar daddy. You don't need a Russian oligarch. But therein lies one of the challenges, because the guys who invest a decent slug of money in a county do expect to have a say in the way the game is run.'

Why wouldn't they? It's not only human nature; it's their money. Better maybe to be a captain or coach under a committee than a capitalist.

What was it Rod Bransgrove said? 'I thought what happened at Hampshire would have been a wake-up call for some counties but it wasn't. They just assume that someone or something will come along.' Well, as Hampshire made evident, someone does. Bransgrove himself came along. At Glamorgan Paul Russell came along. At Headingley Colin Graves stepped in to secure the club. For if English cricket was going to be an eye-catching national sport as well as have a headline-grabbing Test team, it did have to improve its clapped-out grounds and facilities. Living in the past is one thing; sitting in it or queuing several overs for a warm beer is something else. And the investment to finance those improvements had to come from somewhere. It wasn't all going to come from the ECB, even in loans.

The ECB's business model to which the counties are linked, based as it is on international cricket and television rights, remains a precarious one. The free-to-air broadcasters have given no real indication that they're interested in Test cricket – neither the BBC nor ITV bid to televise cricket live when Sky were awarded the rights for 2006 onwards – and with the digital switchover almost upon us we're entering an era of volatility in broadcasting. The ECB successfully saw off attempts to get cricket back on the 'A' list of sports events, those which have to be received by at least 95 per cent of the UK population. But, sports minister Hugh Robertson wrote in a letter to the *Guardian*, the government 'will review the list after the switchover in 2012, by which time the whole landscape will look very different'.

No doubt the ECB lobbyists are already hard at work again, explaining in great detail the financial implications of any policy that restricts the Board's ability to sell their broadcasting rights on an open market. But that Ashes victory in Australia might yet prove to be a double-edged sword. While on the one hand it undoubtedly strengthened the ECB's negotiating position with broadcasters, it also illustrated the national appetite for and the goodwill factor associated with the Ashes brand. The government may decide that everyone should have access to live coverage of it, and not just one broadcaster's subscribers.

Uncertainty over broadcasting revenue is, to me, perhaps the biggest threat facing the counties in the decade to 2020. It's certainly a good reason why they should bury their differences and start taking control of their own destiny. If that means restructuring the ECB so they have their own separate governance, they should go for it, not as a measure of last resort but as a practical, positive way forward for the whole business. As we keep being told, they own the ECB, not the other way round.

A little over 70 years ago, in July 1940, the magazine *Picture Post* illustrated its cover story, 'The British way of life', with a photo of a boy holding a cricket bat, contrasting this with an image of a boy in Hitler

Youth uniform as the representative of the militaristic German way of life. Pure propaganda, of course, and not so much a reflection of the British way of life as of an English way. It carried on a theme that Britain had fostered abroad throughout the 1930s, with leisure and recreation featured prominently on British stands at international exhibitions. At Paris in 1937 cricket was one of several sports, along with football, tennis, golf, angling and also darts, depicted as integral to the country's heritage and the English concept of fair play. Indeed, writes Professor Jonathan Woodham in *Twentieth-Century Design*, 'cricket was a particular conveyor of such ideals, bringing with it notions of green lawns, afternoon tea, and reminiscences of the archetypal village green beside the church. All such ideas represented a projection of national identity distinct from the overt and distinct propagandist outlook of a number of countries… especially Germany and the USSR.'

It's hard to imagine cricket being viewed today as the embodiment of English national identity – a bit multi-cultural, mind – and that's no reflection on cricket. It's more a reflection of England, for England's perception of itself as a nation has changed. I seem to recall historian David Starkey and novelist P. D. James surmising in 2009 whether the sense of England as a nation had almost vanished. Starkey ventured that England had become 'a post nation'. Not if you were waiting for a letter, it hadn't.

Viewing England as an outsider, if that epithet remains apt after 40 years or more living in London, not that living in London is necessarily the same as living in England, I'm not so sure that England as a nation has vanished. It may have lost its way a little; lost some confidence in itself. You see this in government ministers snatching snippets of immigration policy from Australia and education from Canada and Scandinavia, in county chiefs going to India to seek salvation in the IPL. These mix-and-hope-to-match imports strike me as the intellectual balance of payments tilting further into the red. They may be part of a solution but they are not an answer. England is a big nation; it should have ideas of its own, even when it comes to cricket. It is, after all, the land that gave Twenty20 to the world and through that invention brought Australia to its Test-cricketing knees. Or so some would surmise.

While I wouldn't hazard a guess at what the future holds for county cricket, I cannot imagine that it doesn't have one. It is too embedded in what intuitively I sense to be the essence of England: its countryside, its varied landscapes. Not the urban sprawls with all their vitality and poverty, great wealth and immense deprivation, opportunity for some, despair for others. Yes, they are part of England but they are not unique to England. Nor is cricket, but something about cricket is. A something that chimes with what Kipling must have felt when he wrote of building 'from age to age an undefiled heritage'.

You can come to England in April and, if you have the time and some resources, you can get a game of cricket every day probably until September. You don't always have to be a good cricketer; it won't necessarily be the case that the cricket is good. You might find yourself taking the field alongside millionaires, vicars, schoolmasters, a Regius professor or even a rock legend, an accountant and an actor, jump jockeys and journalists, a pig farmer, a cartoonist or two, a chinaman bowler, a white van driver and a West Indian (here you thank the Lord you're on the same side) who was in a quartet with Holding or Roberts or Marshall or one of those guys. If it really is your lucky day you might find yourself walking around the boundary in conversation with a woman with the most wonderful complexion and no conscience.

But you don't have to be a player; you might be a watcher. There was a time, any day from April to September, when you could stroll into a county ground in England for a fiver or a tenner and see some of the best cricketers in the world. Somewhere along the line it all got out of kilter, as if it stopped mattering that people, however few, would want to watch cricket. There were bank holidays when there was no county cricket. B&Q and barbecues filled the vacuum because ironically it was on those bank holidays that the sun often shone.

This isn't nostalgia, simply a few observations. What we don't use we can lose, and if county cricket is to be England's pre-eminent professional summer sport it requires more practical support than a few million website hits. It needs people filling county grounds on a regular basis, and it needs income, be it through gate money, membership, merchandising or partaking in commercial activities. It needs the cricket-loving public, so called, to embrace the county game wholeheartedly and provide it with the same vibrant following they give the England team. The counties themselves have to get their act together, that's true, but whether it's 18 counties or 38, three-format schedules or just the Championship and Twenty20, the county game can't get by on goodwill alone. Goodwill doesn't bring home that much bacon. There has to be a collective effort from everyone who professes to follow this wonderful game. Administrators, committeemen and members; dedicated fans and casual walk-ups; sponsors and advertisers, national and local media; the young, the old, the great and the good, the not so great and the not so good. In other words, cricket lovers of all persuasions working together. It's the nation's heritage you're keeping alive.

INDEX